CHINESE BUZZWORDS

WITH ENGLISH EXPLANATIONS

Second Edition

by *Shanghai Daily*

Better Link Press

Copyright © 2009 Shanghai Press and Publishing Development Company and
Shanghai Daily

This book is edited and designed by the Editorial Committee of *Cultural China* series

Managing Directors: Wang Youbu, Xu Naiqing
Editorial Director: Wu Ying
Editors: Wu Zheng, Meng Tiexia, Wang Yong, Guo Min

Compiled by *Shanghai Daily*
Interior and Cover Design: Zhang Lelu
Computer Typeset: Wang Wei

ISBN: 978-1-60220-406-5

Address any comments about *Chinese Buzzwords (Second Edition)* **to:**
Better Link Press
99 Park Ave
New York, NY 10016
USA
or
Shanghai Press and Publishing Development Company
F 7 Donghu Road, Shanghai, China (200031)
Email: comments_betterlinkpress@hotmail.com

Printed in China by Shanghai Donnelley Printing Co. Ltd.

1 2 3 4 5 6 7 8 9 10

To World Expo 2010
Shanghai China

CONTENTS

FOREWORD

Translating words and phrases from one language into another is never easy. Doing it for a daily newspaper is especially challenging and difficult due to the pressure of deadlines.

Making a tough situation tougher, we are now facing a daily avalanche of new terms, phrases and jargons. They pop up on campuses, in business and cultural circles, among computer geeks and in online BBS and chat rooms.

However, it is an obligation for an English-language newspaper such as Shanghai Daily, which is based in a city where English is not the native language, to render such new Chinese terms into English.

During the process, our editorial staff, both native Chinese and English speakers, came up with the idea of introducing a weekly "Buzzwords" column to answer questions frequently asked by our readers regarding translation of new Chinese terms and phrases.

We planned this column with three purposes: first, to provide a tentative English translation of new Chinese terms and phrases as a reference for our readers; second, to tell our readers what are the latest buzzwords used by locals in their work and daily life; and third, to invite readers to help us generate better English translations of such stylish or trendy Chinese words and phrases.

Since the column first appeared in October 2005, we have been overwhelmed by readers' enthusiastic responses. Some have offered suggestions for alternative renderings of specific terms and phrases, and many others have simply asked for more.

To satisfy our readers' insatiable appetite for knowledge, we decided to compile all the terms and phrases published in our "Buzzwords" column in the past four years into this little book. We hope it may help our readers gain a better understanding of new Chinese words and phrases and serve as a useful reference in their work and daily life.

We present each term first in Chinese and then in pinyin (the Roman alphabet system for Chinese characters). Then, it's followed by its English translation and a short paragraph to explain its basic meaning and usage.

The translation in this book shall never been deemed as perfect, but it's the best try on our side. According to the Chinese idiom " 抛砖引玉 " (throwing out a brick to attract jade), we see our endeavor as throwing out a "brick." We certainly hope that this little book will stoke up the interest and deliberations of some " 骨灰级 " (guru) experts to come up with better renderings.

Meanwhile, as life goes on, new terms and phrases will keep gushing out like water from an eternal fountain. So, we will keep trying to render them into English in a timely manner as we did before.

Peter Zhang
Editor-in-Chief
Shanghai Daily
June 2009

A

AB制 (AB zhì)
AB treat

In China, people tend to call "going Dutch" an "AA treat," meaning dividing the bill equally among all the diners. But now "AB treat" has become a fad among young people as some males now choose to pay a bigger slice of the bill, say 70 percent, while female friends dining with them pay the rest.

阿尔法女孩 (ā ér fǎ nǚ hái)
alpha woman

Alpha women can always outperform men in study, work and sports. So, where there are alpha women, there are beta men.

阿木林 (ā mù lín)
moron

The expression in Shanghai dialect is a transliteration

from the English word. It came into use after foreign powers set up concession areas in the city in the mid–19th century.

阿姨 (ā yí)
IE or Internet Explorer

The Chinese term, which means literally "auntie," has a similar pronunciation with IE (Internet Explorer) and is widely used among Chinese netizens, especially in headlines of BBS posts, to attract people's attention, because ayi sometimes refers to a caring female.

安全岛 (ān quán dǎo)
safety island

Shanghai police are trying to improve traffic facilities to ensure road safety. Safety islands have been built in the middle of some wide roads around the city to offer pedestrians a temporary haven from rushing traffic.

肮三 (āng sān)
indecent, wicked, problematic

Originally, this was Pidgin English meaning "on

sale" in Shanghai dialect. Then it was used to depict substandard or bad quality products. Now, it is often used to describe a person or his/her behavior that is immoral or highly offensive and obnoxious. It may also be used to talk about a bad situation.

拗断 (ǎo duàn)
separate/break away

It can refer to either the breakdown of good relations between a couple, or good friends, or the breakup of a showbiz artist from his or her broker.

拗分族 (ǎo fēn zú)
young extorters

It refers to juvenile delinquents or school bullies who extort money or possessions from young students, usually on their way home.

拗造型 (ǎo zào xíng)
poseur

The Chinese term derives from Shanghai dialect and has become very popular among young people. It describes someone who attempts to achieve a status, look or appeal which they do not have the traits to possess. The Chinese term may also be used as verb to mean someone's acting that way.

奥布 (ào bù)
dirty trick

The term originates from the dialect of southern Fujian Province and means cunning thoughts or methods that are used to reach a certain goal. It was extensively used during the election of local leaders in Taiwan as some candidates were discovered employing unfair or unlawful methods to collect votes in support of particular candidates.

奥特曼 (ào tè màn)
out man

The expression is a transliteration from "Ultraman," a hero in an animated TV series. But these days, many people use it as a transliteration for the English words "out man" to describe "out-dated rubes."

奥运婚 (ào yùn hūn)
Olympic marriage

The 2008 Beijing Olympic Games are not just a party for sports fans but also for many brides and grooms. The number of wedding registrations in Shanghai hit a record on August 8, the opening day of the Games, as many young couples wanted the memorable day as their wedding anniversary.

B

八卦 (bā guà)
gossip, gossipy

Originally the name of an eight-side diagram derived from the famous Chinese classic "I Ching"(*Book of Changes*), it is now often used to describe gossip or gossipy people. Some believe this term first came into use in Hong Kong where the "yin-yang" diagram was frequently used to cover the crucial points of nude models on gossip or porn magazine covers.

八角茴香 (bā jiǎo huí xiāng)
star anise

Star anise is a traditional Chinese herbal medicine or flavoring, which is also known as eight-cornered fennel. Recently there is a buying spree for star anise in some parts of China as media reported that it is an important ingredient of Roche's Tamiflu, a medicine believed to be able to prevent bird flu.

80后 (bā líng hòu)
80's generation

The word refers to those who were born in the 1980s. They are considered to be a self-centered generation who care more about themselves compared with older generations. They are also more willing to try new things, heavily influenced by the Internet and more open to foreign cultures.

八荣八耻 (bā róng bā chǐ)
Eight Do's and Eight Don't's

Chinese President Hu Jintao recently called on the whole nation and particularly young people to adopt the "socialist concept of honor and disgrace," also known as "Eight Do's and Eight Don't's." The list reads: "Love, do not harm the motherland; Serve, don't disserve the people; Uphold science, Don't be ignorant and unenlightened; Work hard, don't be lazy and hate work; Be united and help each other, don't gain benefits at the expense of others; Be honest and trustworthy, don't be profit-mongering at the expense of your values; Be disciplined and law-abiding, don't be unruly and lawless; Respect plain living and hard struggle, don't wallow in luxuries and pleasures."

霸王条款 (bà wáng tiáo kuǎn)
big-brother term, despot term

The terms in a commercial contract brainworked to ensure one party's absolute advantage over the other party, usually the client, in transaction are called "*bawang tiaokuan*" or "terms of the overlord."

白骨精 (bái gǔ jīng)
office elite

This is the name of a siren in the famous Chinese novel *Journey to the West*. But, today it is also used as a new title for white-collar office workers who excel in their career. Instead of the "White-Bone Demon," the three Chinese characters in this term refers to white-collar, backbone and elite, respectively, in its new usage.

白客 (bái kè)
online security guard

The phrase, which literally means "white clan" in Chinese, is the opposite of "black clan" or hacker. It refers to professionals who fight hackers in order to protect people's information security in the online world. It's not unusual that some of the online security guards are former hackers.

白色污染 (bái sè wū rǎn)
white pollution

This term refers to pollution caused by litter of used plastic bags, polystyrene cups, food containers and paper.

白托 (bái tuō)
daytime care service

The term refers to a government project aiming to improve community care for senior citizens. The community center will serve the elderly lunches and dinners and organize some recreational activities for them during the day.

白眼狼 (bái yǎn láng)
ungrateful soul

The phrase literally translates as a "white–eyed wolf," but it actually means an ungrateful person. Chinese tend to deem both "white eye" (eyes with too much white) and "wolf" as derogatory terms.

白纸男 (bái zhǐ nán)
virgin man

This term, which translates literally as "white-paper man," refers to those men who have never dated a girlfriend or never had any love experience before. Chinese tend to use the term "white paper" to mean anything that has never been tapped or violated.

百搭 (bǎi dā)
all-matching, joker, Jack of all trades

If a piece of clothing or accessory goes easily with other clothing of any color or style or an electronics part or device is compatible with all other parts or devices needed for a complete set it is an all-matching case. The phrase also means "joker" in a card game that can be used to trump or substitute any other cards.

百搭简历 (bǎi dā jiǎn lì)
all-fitting resume

It is a kind of resume that job seekers prepare in such an ambiguous way that it apparently meets the requirements of many kinds of job.

百搭药 (bǎi dā yào)
panacea

Many people take antibiotics whenever they get a fever, cough, or slight headache, as if antibiotics cure all. The state has recently banned doctors from indiscriminately prescribing antibiotics for their patients.

百恼汇 (bǎi nǎo huì)
middle-age crisis

The term has a similar pronunciation to "Buynow," the name of a computer market, in Chinese. Meaning "a host of worries" it is now used to describe the lifestyle crisis facing many middle-aged people.

摆乌龙 (bǎi wū lóng)
go wrong, botch up

This term usually refers to an own goal in a soccer game, but it is now used frequently to mean something goes wrong or someone botches up a seemingly good plan.

摆噱头 (bǎi xuè tóu)
sales stunt, publicity stunt

This term is frequently used by people to describe the publicity tricks that a business uses to promote a product that more often than not will turn out to be expensive trash.

百元周 (bǎi yuán zhōu)
100-yuan week

Some white-collar workers in Shanghai have started to change their bourgeois lifestyle for a thriftier one in face of the ongoing financial crisis. Some put online posters among popular BBS communities to call on people to control their expenditure within 100 yuan from Monday to Friday, including costs on food, traffic, entertainment, shopping and sport activities.

败家子 (bài jiā zǐ)
black sheep

The Chinese term has a narrower meaning than the English one. The Chinese term only refers to a member of a family who is undesirable.

版主（斑竹）(bān zhú)
BBS moderator

This term is frequently used among netizens. The Chinese term in the brackets is actually a rib tickler applied here mainly because it shares a similar pronunciation to the official term. Originally, it is the name of the Mottled Bamboo.

半唐蕃 (bàn táng fān)
half–Chinese

This is a Cantonese term that refers to people, behavior, manners, language and culture that are half–Chinese and half–foreign.

半糖夫妻 (bàn táng fū qī)
weekend couple

This term translates literally as "half–sugar husband and wife." It refers to couples who live separately five work days of a week and only spend the weekend to-gether to keep their relationship fresh and exciting.

帮帮忙 (bāng bāng máng)
come on, give me a break

The colloquial expression serves as a mild request for help in Mandarin, but in Shanghai dialect, it is an admonition before arguing against a remark someone has made.

帮倒忙 (bāng dào máng)
disservice, a bad turn

The Chinese term, which can be translated literally as "a reverse of help," actually means an act intended to help that turns out badly.

榜单 (bǎng dān)
top list

It is a list of top players in terms of their fame, popularity, income, authority or skills.

膀爷 (bǎng yé)
topless man

The word literally means "shoulder grandpa" in Chinese. It refers to men who like to walk on the street topless during summer. Having long been criticized in the media and by the public, the phenomenon almost disappeared from Beijing streets during the Olympics but has not gone completely.

傍大款 (bàng dà kuǎn)
live off a moneybags

It is used frequently in daily talk in a derogative way to describe the phenomenon of a woman trying her best to marry or live off a rich man.

棒杀 (bàng shā)
crucify, ruthlessly repudiate

The Chinese term means literally to bludgeon someone to death. In everyday conservation, it is often used to mean criticizing someone harshly.

包机 (bāo jī)
charter flight

The flights are specially arranged for travelers. This year, both sides across the Taiwan Strait have designed six carriers to make 36 round–trip charter flights for Spring Festival, the most important traditional Chinese festival.

保送生 (bǎo sòng shēng)
direct admission student

According to a direct admission program in China, a small number of high school graduates can be enrolled by colleges and universities without having to sit the entrance examinations. Such students are usually selected for their high grades and good conduct.

保鲜膜 (bǎo xiān mó)
cling film

China's health authority recently conducted a spot check on cling film wrapping after receiving reports that a chemical linked to cancer is in some products.

保质期 (bǎo zhì qī)
shelf life or best-before date

Shanghai health authorities have employed a team of volunteer food inspectors to check whether food or medicines are sold after the expiry dates or for other quality problems as part of nationwide efforts to ensure safe food and drugs.

抱抱团 (bào bào tuán)
free huggers

Some people offer free hugs for strangers in streets of big Chinese cities, such as Shanghai and Beijing. They hold signs saying "Care from strangers" and "No to cold shoulders" in Chinese and the words of "Free hugs" in English. The huggers say "free hugs will bring people closer."

爆场 (bào chǎng)
raise the roof

More often than not, promotions that offer deep discounts for well-established brands will attract a huge crowd that raises the roof.

爆发 (bào fā)
sudden metamorphosis, sudden eruption in form

The Chinese term translates literally "burst," "outburst" or "eruption." But it is often used to describe a sudden improvement in a person or team's performance.

B

暴利税 (bào lì shuì)
windfall profit tax

China has started levying tax on outrageous profits oil businesses reap in the hope that it can make up for the losses these monopolies cause to disadvantaged groups and public welfare services.

爆料 (bào liào)
tip off, blow the whistle

Many news media nowadays rely heavily on tip-offs from their stringers or street tipsters to scoop some exclusive news. They usually offer the tipsters a handsome reward in cash. Seeing this trend, some laid-off workers and migrants have turned tipping into a business to eke out a living.

爆棚 (bào péng)
packed, a box-office hit

The word is believed to have made its way into Mandarin from Hong Kong via the Guangdong dialect. *Bao* literally means burst and *peng*, a shed or shack.

贝多芬 (bèi duō fēn)
back–baring lady

This phrase is quite popular among college students who use it to refer to those young women who wear fashionable clothes that bare as much of their back as possible. This Chinese term is actually a translation of the name of Ludwig van Beethoven, but the first character of the term sounds like "back," the second means "more" and the last "fragrance."

奔奔族 (bēn bēn zú)
rushing clan

It refers to those people between 20–30 years old born into a common family who are highly dependent on the Internet for social life but highly independent in thinking, highly pressed by financial burdens but highly likely to become a "card slave" or "house slave."

本本族 (běn běn zú)
carless drivers

This term refers to those who have driving licenses but seldom have opportunities to practise their skills because they don't have their own cars. They are also called "road killer" as their lack of experience can easily cause traffic accidents.

本草纲目 (běn cǎo gāng mù)
dumb and annoying

It is an expression popular with youngsters when they call a person stupid, noisy, and dull. The expression, borrowed from the title of an ancient Chinese medicine encyclopedia, *Compendium of Materia Medica*, plays on the four Chinese characters 笨 (stupid), 吵 (noisy), 戆 (simple-minded), and 木 (unresponsive), which sound similar to the title.

本命年 (běn mìng nián)
year of fate

In ancient China, people believed that a person's fate was determined at birth, so the zodiac year of one's birth would be one's "year of fate." To fend off the default "bad luck" in such a year, people tend to wear red underwear, red waistbands and red bracelets. According to the Chinese lunar calendar, this year is the "year of fate" for people who were born in the Year of the Pig.

崩盘 (bēng pán)
market crash, business collapse

This term is often used to mean the stock market crash. But it may also be used to mean any kind of business collapse or even the breakup of a relationship.

蹦迪 (bèng dí)
disco dancing

Dancing discos in nightclubs or bars is a popular entertainment among young people who want to get some exercise and find a way of catharsis. But many nightclubs are often involved in complaints by nearby residents for the noise created by them, such as loud music and blaring car horns.

避风头 (bì fēng tóu)
dodge the brunt, lie low

The Chinese term translates literally "to dodge the brunt of the wind." One way to stay out of the trouble and avoid being caught is to avoid the hot track and lie low.

毕婚族 (bì hūn zú)
marry–upon–graduation

The new expression refers to those young people who marry immediately after graduating from college. However, they need more time and experience to get weaned off the pampering of their parents.

编外 (biān wài)
outside the staff establishment

Under the planned economy, the government assigned to every work unit in China an authorized staff establishment or manning scale. Some still do. But often such work units or government departments need to hire people outside the fixed establishment and such employees usually are denied some privileges or perks for their counterparts who are within the staff establishment.

边缘人 (biān yuán rén)
marginal man

It refers to a person who lives in the marginal area of a social sector or a profession. It can also be used for a person who straddles two cultures in society.

便当 (biàn dāng)
bentou

The term is a translation of the Japanese word for the takeaway boxed lunch and in Chinese it literally means "convenient." On the Chinese mainland, people usually call it hefan, meaning "boxed meal" or lunch box, while in Taiwan, a growing number of people now use the term "bentou."

便利贴女孩 (biàn lì tiē nǚ hái)
post-it girl

It refers to those kind-hearted, usually plain-looking young women at a workplace who are always ready to help others and then almost immediately forgotten after the help. They are like the post-it notes people use and then throw away.

变脸 (biàn liǎn)
face-lift, change the look

The term originally refers to Sichuan Change Art, but now means cosmetic surgery. It also refers to the complete renovation of certain places or buildings. Shanghai's Wujiang Road, which is famous for its snack vendors, will receive a face-lift and become a fashion street in the near future.

飙车 (biāo chē)
drag racing

Living a better life than before, some Chinese youngsters are infatuated with drag racing. Recently the Chinese media reported that some people drove their Coach Builder Cars at a dangerous speed racing around Beijing's ring roads. The police have arrested two youngsters in their 20s for driving at nearly 150 kilometers an hour in downtown streets.

标题党 (biāo tí dǎng)
sensational headline writers

Sensational headline writers always produce headings that can hardly be substantiated by the following text. As the headlines usually attract readers' attention before they read the stories, now headline writers are even being hired by some malicious programmers to seduce netizens to click on files containing viruses.

别苗头 (bié miáo toú)
vie, compete for favor

The phrase comes from Shanghai dialect and is translated into mandarin phonetically. It's an informal way of saying competition and usually indicates some sly moves on both sides.

病房 (bìng fáng)
defective house

The Chinese term means literally wards in a hospital. Now, the "sickroom" is also used to refer to a house or an apartment with quality defects.

Bo播报 (Bo bō bào)
multimedia newspaper

The term refers to a new form of electronic "newspaper," which combines text, photos, graphics, audio and video. One can also search background data and cross reference with this news platform.

播客 (bō kè)
podcaster

The word, a hybrid of "Ipod" and "broadcast," refers to those who combine a group of technologies to distribute audio and video files over the Internet. Readers may receive podcasts of this buzzword column online or download them to an MP3 player from www.shanghaidaily.com.

玻璃悬崖 (bō lí xuán yá)
glass cliff

Chinese are now quick to introduce new English terms. This glass cliff is one example. It means a senior job or important project, particularly one given to a woman, with a high risk of failure.

搏出位 (bó chū wèi)
steal the spotlight, draw attention

It refers to sometimes a despicable way of seeking attention from others or the public.

博斗 (bó dòu)
blog bickering

The term is a homonym of the Chinese word "fight," but it conjoins two Chinese characters that can mean "blog" and "fight," respectively. So, the phrase refers to Netizens tilting at each other on their blogs.

博客圈 (bó kè quān)
blogosphere

Blogosphere refers to a special community culture

resulting from the close interconnecting between weblogs and frequent interacting and communication among bloggers.

搏票 (bó piào)
ticket struggle

Train tickets are hard to get when millions of college students and migrant workers head home for the Spring Festival every year. Obtaining a train ticket has inevitably been turned into a tough struggle. People have to brave the chilly wind and line up outside ticket offices all night long, which still won't guarantee them a home-bound ticket.

布波族 (bù bō zú)/ 波波族 (bō bō zú)
bo-bos

The word is a shorthand for Bourgeois-Bohemians, which refers to the young who have the hybrid characteristics of the 1960s hippies and 1980s yuppies. They are well-educated and barely bound by tradition, prefer fashionable clothes and modern appliances, but are always moving their home between cities and the countryside to avoid a stereotyped life.

不感冒 (bù gǎn mào)
uninterested, peeved

Having no flu (*bu ganmao*)? That's good. But don't take the Chinese term verbatim. In colloquial conservations, this term means that one is uninterested in or even peeved by something others said or did. So don't talk about Tamiflu when there's no flu threat in sight.

不灵光 (bù líng guāng)
no good

The frequently used expression has a wide range of meanings from a gadget being at fault, a plan bearing no fruit, to a fad losing popularity.

不粘锅 (bù zhān guō)
diner-out

The Chinese phrase, which literally means Teflon cooking utensils, is now often used to describe those young people who always eat out and stay away from their kitchens. It's because either they are too busy with their job or don't bother to do the cooking.

不折腾 (bù zhē teng)
don't stir up turmoil

The term is colloquial and widely used to discourage someone from getting restless due to illness, worry or from just messing around. But when it was quoted by Chinese President Hu Jintao in his recent report, it referred to acts that would disturb society's normal life. So, "don't stir up (political or social) turmoil" reflects people's desire for peace and harmony.

C

擦边球 (cā biān qiú)
rule–bending act

The term means an edge ball in games such as table tennis, which is a tricky play but one that scores. Now it is often used to describe someone who achieves his/her goals by bending the rules without being caught or by maneuvering in the grey area of the system.

彩虹族 (cǎi hóng zú)
rainbow clan

Rainbow is seen as colorful and cheerful. So, this term refers to people who are good at finding a balance between work and life. They pay attention to diet, health and quality of life without sacrificing career advancement.

菜鸟 (cài niǎo)
rookie, novice

The Chinese term literally means young birds which

have just begun to learn to fly. Lack of skill and experience often makes them faltering and an easy target for their enemies or rivals.

蚕茧族 (cán jiǎn zú)
cocoon clan

Quite a few young office workers opt to stay at home and do things alone as much as possible to shun social activities at free time, turning their residence into a cocoon.

残念 (cán niàn)
letdown, too bad

Young people these days often use this term to express disappointment when they fail to obtain something they desire. It is derived from the Japanese phrase "zan nen."

藏镜人 (cáng jìng rén)
string puller

A person who makes use of others to reach his or her own purpose, without being identified as the person behind it all.

藏牌车 (cáng pái chē)
plate-hiding vehicle

Some drivers cover their vehicle plates with papers, mud or other objects so that they can violate traffic rules without being caught by police or traffic cameras.

草割 (cǎo gē)
hands down, easy win

When one man is much stronger and more skillful than his rival in a fight, he can beat the latter as handily as "cutting grass."

草根艺人 (cǎo gēn yì rén)
mudsill artiste

The past few years have seen quite a few self-taught artistes, particularly stand-up comedians, around the country rise to the national fame. The Chinese term translates literally "artiste from the grassroots." Although they practice a "low" art form, they are getting high ratings and laughs.

草莓族 (cǎo méi zú)
strawberry clan

This term refers to students fresh from school. Just like the fresh fruit, they usually have a good appearance, but are easily perishable as they lack work experience or the moxie to fight pressure.

草食男 (cǎo shí nán)
herbivorous man

It refers to men who are gentle and very polite toward women. But they rarely take the initiative or an aggressive approach to court the female they love. Instead, they tend to keep a lukewarm relationship with them.

草台 (cǎo tái)
makeshift; low-quality

This term usually refers to a makeshift stage used for providing entertainment performances in rural areas. Now it is widely used to mean anything that is makeshift, or of low quality.

C

蹭健族 (cèng jiàn zú)
gym hanger-on

The term refers to people who seek coupons or other opportunities to use gymnasiums for free. They tend to occupy the facilities for a long time, making themselves a nuisance in many gyms.

蹭停族 (cèng tíng zú)
free parking tribe

The expression refers to those drivers who try to park their car in a place, such as school compounds, that charges no parking fees.

叉腰肌 (chā yāo jī)
tangential excuse

The term means literally iliopsoas—the great flexor muscle of the hip joint. It has become one of the hottest buzzwords in China after Xie Yalong, China's senior soccer official, recently used it to criticize the women's national soccer team, blaming their failure at the Olympic Games on their weak iliopsoas muscles. Most Netizens believe it's an extremely tangential excuse cited by Xie to avoid the blame.

拆烂污 (chāi làn wū)
mess up knowingly

The phrase originally means to suffer diarrhea in Shanghai dialect. Later it has come to mean an intentional act of muddling along and then looking on without offering a helping hand when problems arise.

长跑令 (cháng pǎo lìng)
long jog requirement

The Chinese Ministry of Education has asked students across the country to take a long jog every morning from October 26 through to April 30 in 2008, in an attempt to improve their physical condition. Under the plan, grade-five and grade-six students will run 1,000 meters per day, middle school students 1,500 meters, and high school and university students 2,000 meters. The compulsory jogging has attracted protests from parents who worry their children will be too tired after the morning exercises to focus on their studies.

抄底游 (chāo dǐ yóu)
rock-bottom price travel

As many airlines and hotels have started to cut their prices amid the global financial downturn, some

Chinese take advantage of the opportunity to embark on overseas travel at much lower costs than before.

超额配售 (chāo é pèi shòu)
green shoe option

A provision in an underwriting agreement which allows the underwriter to purchase additional initial public offering shares at the original price after the shares begin trading. The name comes from the fact that Green Shoe Company was the first to grant such an option to underwriters. It also called over−allotment provision.

超 A 货 (chāo A huò)
AAA−grade replica

The term refers to high−end replicas of luxury brand products. With almost the exact look of outside and interior and even fake certificate IDs, they are nightmares for luxury brand product manufacturers.

超级飚涨 (chāo jí biāo zhǎng)
super spike

It means the unprecedented and extremely rapid rise

in the price of a commodity, such as the skyrocketing price increase in oil in the past few months.

潮人 (cháo rén)
trendsetter

Those who do not follow a fashion or fad in a blind way but have original idea about how to be in, as in the style of dressing and making up, fall into this type of trendsetters.

炒婚 (chǎo hūn)
wedding fanfare

China's champion gymnast Yang Wei disputes online criticism of his ostentatious wedding ceremony, saying love for his bride Yang Yun was his focus and some of the luxurious aspects were from sponsoring businesses.

炒作 (chǎo zuò)
sensationalize

It is a popular way to promote a film, a star or anyone who wants to be famous. For example, you may hear a film's star fall in love during the production, which is actually used to attract more attention to the movie.

车搭子 (chē dā zi)
carpoolers

This term refers to people who organize carpools for convenience as they live in the same or neighboring residential areas. The car owner will charge a fee to set off the fuel cost. But local authorities frown upon the practice, believing it blurs the line between carpools and unlicensed taxi services.

车友会 (chē yǒu huì)
motorists' club

As the number of private cars keeps growing in the country recently, the clubs of motorists of different auto brands have mushroomed. The club members, mostly young white-collar workers, attend club parties, take long driving journeys together from time to time, and share sweet and bitter experiences with their cars.

成分献血 (chéng fèn xiàn xuě)
component blood donation

Component blood donation is a specialized service

where donors are hooked up to automated machines which separate the donated blood into all its various components, so rather than donating whole blood, a donor has the option to donate only some blood components while retaining others.

城管 (chéng guǎn)
urban management official

Urban management officials are supposed to keep illegal vendors off the street, among other jobs. Some officials in Shanghai have been equipped with safety equipment, including anti-puncture vests and steel helmets, to guard against possible violent violators.

城市补丁 (chéng shì bǔ dīng)
run-down neighborhoods

The Chinese term literally means "city patches," which is a reference to an urban area marked by crowded and dirty run-down housing, against the backdrop of spanking new high-rises.

城乡结合部 (chéng xiāng jié hé bù)
rural–urban fringe zone

Millions of migrants flowing into the city every year have turned the boundary zone outside the urban proper into bustling areas where the migrants can find affordable housing and relatively easy access to their work in downtown districts. Sometimes, however, the term has a pejorative intonation as it's often deemed as a synonym of the hotbed for crimes and unlicensed shoddy products.

城中村 (chéng zhōng cūn)
shantytown

A recent residential collapse in Zhengzhou, Henan Province, that killed four people raised concerns about the safety of residents in dilapidated and illegally built houses in urban areas.

吃瘪 (chī biē)
eat humble pie, eat boiled crow

This is a widely used term in the Shanghai dialect, which means to be forced to accept a defeat resentfully or admit one's faults in humiliating circumstances.

吃豆腐 (chī dòu fu)
take advantage of, come on to

Eating tofu, as this Chinese phrase literally means, is not just common at dinner tables, but also very popular in daily conversations among locals. But in conservations, this phrase usually means a man takes advantage of or comes on to a woman. It may also be used among people of the same sex, when one bullies another verbally or even physically.

吃空饷 (chī kōng xiǎng)
ghost payroll scheme

In a scandal spotlighted by Chinese media, an Inner Mongolia human resource official used her position to allocate her 14-year-old daughter a job, which caused an embezzlement of three years of salary by misrepresenting the payroll.

吃软饭 (chī ruǎn fàn)
Kept man

It is a deprecating expression to refer to a man who depends on his girlfriend or wife for a living. The Chinese phrase literally translates as "eating soft rice."

吃素的 (chī sù de)
pushover, sucker, basket case

The term usually is used to call anyone who is a vegetarian. But in colloquial Chinese, it may also refer to someone who is an easy target or easy prey or who is weak and useless.

吃药 (chī yào)
screw up someone

It means more than the literal definition of taking a medication in colloquial conversation. It refers to the act of using a trick to make someone look embarrassed or get into trouble.

赤脚律师 (chì jiǎo lǜ shī)
bare-foot lawyer

The term refers to "grassroots" consultants offering legal assistance to farmers. They usually have a secondary education background and some basic knowledge about the law but are not certified lawyers.

充电 (chōng diàn)
recharge

Borrowed from the common practice of recharging batteries, this expression is now often used figuratively to mean reeducation and vocational training.

抽条 (chōu tiáo)
shoot up, give short weight

Based on the phenomenon of plants sprouting in spring, this term has been used to describe kids reaching puberty and beginning to shoot up. But now it is also used to mean a business fraud of giving customers short weight by randomly taking away small amount of products from large packs.

臭美 (chòu měi)
show off, be ostentatious

The Chinese term means to show off one's beauty, possessions, talent or connections in a pretentious way.

出花头 (chū huā tóu)
novel scheme or funky idea, play hanky-panky

This Shanghainese parlance means to introduce some new and funky plans or ideas. But it can also be used to mean someone's playing hanky-panky.

出气筒 (chū qì tǒng)
punching bag

The colloquial expression in Chinese means a person who becomes a target for others to vent their anger or criticism at, though sometimes as a scapegoat for another one who deserves it.

出位 (chū wèi)
overstep the mark

A fresh college graduate has been censured for "overstepping the mark" after she included her sexy photos in her resume, hoping to impress a future employer. The term may also be used to describe a married person who has been involved in extra-marital affairs.

触电 (chù diàn)
flick appearance, thrill

The term was first used to describe a person who acts for the first time in a movie on the sideline of his or her profession. Now it applies to whoever gives it a try on TV or theatrical stages or in any business related to entertainment and high-tech outside their regular job. It also means the thrill you feel when excited or surprised.

穿帮 (chuān bāng)
blow one's cover

The colloquial expression refers to a trick involving two or more frauds that bombs when one of them takes a misstep. The Chinese term means literally that toes are exposed as soon as the upper of shoes is worn out.

穿小鞋 (chuān xiǎo xié)
make someone walk in tight shoes, make it hot for

To walk in tight, toe-pinching shoes is uncomfortable or even painful. The term, which literally means "wearing undersized small shoes," refers to the act of making things hard for someone usually out of ill intention and revenge.

穿衣经 (chuān yī jīng)
dressing manual

Many newspapers and magazines these days run a special column discussing the trendy, and mostly correct, ways of getting dressed.

穿越小说 (chuān yuè xiǎo shuō)
back-in-time novel

It refers to those novels that feature a modern-era hero or heroine who is thrown back to an ancient time and relives the well-known historical events, which however are spiced with supernatural and romantic plots.

创新型国家 (chuàng xīn xíng guó jiā)
innovation-oriented country

President Hu Jintao outlined China's strategy to become an innovation-oriented country in 15 years during a science and technology conference in Beijing.

纯净水 (chún jìng shuǐ)
post without content

The term translates verbatim to "purified water," but it

is often used to describe those online posts that contain little substantial content. It is related to another Chinese term *guanshui* (irrigation) in its literal sense, referring to Web bloggers uploading tons of nonsense to earn more online credits.

糙饭糕 (cī fàn gāo)
wacky, irritating girl

The expression, which literally means a kind of traditional Chinese snack made of sticky rice, is a play on the three Chinese characters in the phrase, meaning someone who is wacky, irritating and pesky. It usually refers to girls.

次级贷款 (cì jí dài kuǎn)
subprime loans

The risk of subprime loans, those offered to homebuyers who do not qualify for market interest rates because of their credit history, is being felt across the United States and rippling over the whole world. Also called B-paper mortgages in comparison to A-paper ones, they carry a rate higher than A-papers due to the increased risk.

次生灾害 (cì shēng zāi hài)
secondary disaster

Disasters or problems that follow or are generated by another disaster, such as a landslide, flash flood or epidemic in the wake of an earthquake.

聪明行动族 (cōng míng xíng dòng zú)
smart mob

See " 快闪暴走族 "(kuài shǎn bào zǒu zú) on page 113.

丛林肉 (cóng lín ròu)
bushmeat

This Chinese term is a translation of the English word "bushmeat," meaning wildlife killed by commercial or subsistence hunters. The use of and trade in bushmeat is now believed to be a key cause of the drastic decline of wild animal populations.

粗口 (cū kǒu)
four-letter word

Dirty words used to express annoyance. Chinese film

director Feng Xiaogang said some four-letter words to a female reporter during an interview. According to media reports, this was not the first time Feng has offered such words.

醋溜族 (cù liū zú)
trendy clan

A group of metropolitan youth is happily caught in the dilemma of following trend and freeing themselves from restrictions. They like brassy appearances but hate neat dressing; like making money but love spending beyond their means; and long for romance but dread responsibilities. The phrase comes from a cartoon series by a Taiwan artist.

存款准备金 (cún kuǎn zhǔn bèi jīn)
reserve requirement

The term means the proportion of deposits a bank, by law, must keep in cash or place with the central bank. It is an important tool for monetary policy, as a higher reserve requirement means fewer funds are available to a bank for lending purposes.

C

搓衣板 (cuō yī bǎn)
thin as a lath

The Chinese term literally means a washing board with wavy grooves. Now it is used jokingly or derogatorily to mean a person, especially a female model, who is as thin as a lath, since their chest case looks very much like a washing board.

D

搭车涨价 (dā chē zhǎng jià)
hitchhike price rise, piggyback price hike
Chinese officials say they will try to prevent some
businesses from willfully raising prices of their products
that are tangential or totally unrelated to the recent fuel
price rise approved by the central government.

达人 (dá rén)
pro, doyen
This term refers to someone who is a pro, doyen or even
an established authority in a specific field of knowledge.
Young people tend to use this term more frequently and
particularly in their online communication.

打底衫 (dǎ dǐ shān)
backing shirt
It refers to the shirt, usually with solid colors and simple
styles, that is worn immediately under an outfit or suit

to set the latter off.

打飞的 (dǎ fēi dī)
hail air taxi

Some people take planes as ordinary taxis to some-where simply for shopping or an examination. People jokingly call it "hailing an air taxi." For example, more than 200 students from a city in southwest China took planes to Hong Kong during the National Day holidays to take the American Scholastic Aptitude Test, one equivalent of China's college entrance examination.

打鸡血 (dǎ jī xuě)
get excited, be stimulated

The word literally means injecting chicken blood, a fad in the late 1960s in China as a way to boost one's health. Now, it is often used to describe someone get-ting excited or stimulated.

打水漂 (dǎ shuǐ piāo)
down the drain, a wasted effort

The term literally means playing ducks and drakes, or skipping stones along the water. But when it is used figuratively, it means that money and effort a person spent has been totally wasted and can't be recovered, just like the stones in the children's game.

打铁 (dǎ tiě)
write a post

It refers to Netizens' comparing an article, especially one worth reading. The phrase translates literally "iron forging," which sounds the same as "writing a post" in Chinese.

大跌眼镜 (dà diē yǎn jìng)
glasses dropper

This Chinese term vividly describes a situation where you're so stunned by something that the glasses fall from the bridge of your nose. Of course, your glasses-dropping could also be caused by the fact that your idea or prediction about something is proved to be wrong as wrong could ever be.

大肚子经济 (dà dù zi jīng jì)
pregnancy economy

Pregnant women have become a force in propelling today's economy as a result of a new baby boom in China. The pregnancy economy consists of child care products, maternity clothing, yoga or health care courses designed for mothers-to-be and particular support services during maternal confinement.

大非 / 小非 (dà fēi /xiǎo fēi)
big/small non-tradable stock

The big non-tradable shares account for five to ten percent of the stock capital and are tradable two years after the reshuffling is completed while the small ones account for less than five percent of the capital and are tradable one year after the reform of stock right is completed.

大佬 (dà lǎo)
big brother, doyen

The Chinese term is most frequently used in Cantonese dialect films, which means "big brother" or doyen. It is not necessarily derogative.

大拿 (dà ná)
big shot, final say

The originally dialectal expression in north China now is commonly used to refer to someone in an organization or a family that has the final say.

大起大落 (dà qǐ dà luò)
boom and bust

Companies that pursue short-term profits without a vision for sustainable development tend to face drastic fluctuation in their performance. The Chinese government is moderating its economic policies to avoid a "boom-and-bust" in the country's micro-economy.

大师杯网球赛 (dà shī bēi wǎng qiú sài)
Tennis Masters Cup

It has become a major sport event in Shanghai. World No.1 Roger Federer said:" For me, this is like a Grand Slam. I came here not knowing if I can play, and I went through all the therapy just to really show people also how much this event really means to me."

大胃王 (dà wèi wáng)
King/Queen of Eating

Miyuki Iwata, a "Queen of Eating" from Japan, has a gargantuan appetite that she puts to full effect at eating competitions around the world. She won the Asia Eating Contest final in Shanghai on May 28, 2006.

大五 (dà wǔ)
dependent college graduate

The expression refers to those university graduates in Chinese cities who live off their parents several months or even a few years after their graduation. This Chinese term is coined to mean the "fifth year in university," implying someone "overstaying" his or her college life.

大小非减持 (dà xiǎo fēi jiǎn chí)
sale of non-tradable shares

China has been actively, and cautiously, encouraging the reform of the system of non-tradable shares in listed companies, as such stocks pose potential damage to the healthy growth of the country's securities markets.

大小人 (dà xiǎo rén)
kidult

The Chinese term which translates literally "adult-aged child" derives from the English word "kidult," a portmanteau of "kid" and "adult." The term refers to middle-aged people who refuse to be denied the freedom and pleasure of youth by doing or buying things designed for children.

带病提拔 (dài bìng tí bá)
promote problematic official

China calls for a strict appraisal of government officials to avoid promoting problematic ones, such as those who are involved in corruption cases.

待机消费 (dài jī xiāo fèi)
optimal buy

This Chinese phrase comprises two parts, the first meaning literally the "standby mode" of a mobile phone and the second part "consumption." Since the first part can also be interpreted as "waiting for an opportunity" in Chinese, this phrase is now used to mean "consumption at an optimum time," such as purchasing consumer goods during a sales or promotion season.

It's the opposite of "impulsive purchase."

代课族 (dài kè zú)
surrogate student

In some Chinese universities, a group of students are earning a fat income by attending classes to answer the roll call and take notes on behalf of "client students" from either the same college or outside institutes.

代排族 (dài pái zú)
hired queuer

People, usually migrants from rural areas and jobless citizens, are hired to queue up for train tickets and hospital appointment tickets in large cities in return for a pittance.

袋鼠爸爸 (dài shǔ bà bà)
kangaroo dad

It refers to a dad who takes care of his child as diligently as a mother. In particular, it refers to a dad who often has skin-to-skin care of his baby to show the intimacy of a loving dad.

袋鼠军团 (dài shǔ jūn tuán)
socceroos

The Chinese term means "troops of kangaroos" literally. It's the nickname of the Australian national soccer team.

带薪创业 (dài xīn chuàng yè)
official-to-businessman switch

It refers to a policy in Xianyang City, Shaanxi Province, which encourages its government officials to become entrepreneurs. According to the policy, the government will keep paying those officials 100 percent of their salaries for the first three years when they start their own businesses. It's regarded as one of the ways to streamline overstaffed government offices.

带薪郁闷假 (dài xīn yù mèn jià)
paid distress day–off

It's a newly introduced paid holiday provided by some Chinese companies. In a year, an employee is allowed a day off for no reason, as long as he or she feels distressed. Under this arrangement, the company pays the person's wage for that day.

蛋白质 (dàn bái zhì)
lunatic jerk

The online jargon has nothing to do with protein, which is meant literally by the Chinese term. Actually, it is a coinage from three different Chinese characters that describe those who are dull and insane.

刀下美人 (dāo xià měi rén)
man–made beauty

This Chinese phrase derives from the title of a 1929 Chinese movie "the Beauty Under the Blade." Now it refers to "man–made beauties" who have gained their looks through surgery.

倒闭网络公司 (dǎo bì wǎng luò gōng sī)
dot-bomb

This term simply means any dot.com companies that are going down the drain or have failed.

倒按揭 (dào àn jiē)
reverse mortgage

Shanghai has been considering the introduction of a reverse mortgage program to help cope with the growing problem of an aging society. The program, also referred to as a home equity conversion loan, first appeared in New Jersey of the United States more than 20 years ago. It was designed to allow seniors to access the equity in their homes.

倒春寒 (dào chūn hán)
cold snap in spring

Spring has come, but from time to time people still may experience cold snaps. It's a common weather phenomenon in Shanghai. People now, however, tend to use this term to depict unexpected setbacks in a booming business.

道德督察 (dào dé dū chá)
moral police

This term describes public opinion attacks on real estate tycoons who refused to donate much to the quake zone in Sichuan.

道德扶贫 (dào dé fú pín)
moral poverty relief

In reporting the recent melamine-laced milk scandal in China, some media point out that the government and all social sectors in the country should not only pay attention to the material poverty in rural areas, but also their moral poverty.

道路百慕大 (dào lù bǎi mù dà)
Terrestrial Bermuda Triangle

Some local media use the phrase to refer to several street crossings in downtown Shanghai that often make drivers confused about which lane to take, like the one at Wujiaochang shopping area.

得来速 (dé lái sù)
drive-thru

McDonald's and KFC have opened drive-thru restaurants in Shanghai.

得体 (dé tí)
dirty

This Chinese phrase originally meant appropriate, decent and in good taste. But since it sounds like the English word "dirty," the phrase is now often used by Netizens to describe anyone who keeps an amiable facade but harbors a vicious heart.

低调 (dī diào)
stay under the radar, keep a low profile

The Chinese phrase literally means low tone. However, it often refers to some people's desire to keep a low profile or to stay under the radar. Some tycoons, who are listed in the 2006 Forbes 400 richest on the mainland, said they will keep a low profile as usual to avoid attracting public attention.

低碳族 (dī tàn zú)
low–CO₂ clan

This refers to the group of conservationists and nature lovers who try to minimize carbon dioxide emissions in daily life, for example, switching off PCs when not using them, shunning goods with excessive packaging, and rejecting the use of plastic bags.

地方粮票 (dì fāng liáng piào)
local policy

The Chinese term literally means local food ration coupons that were widely used in the 1960s when there was a food shortage. Now the term means any policy that's applicable only in a specific locality.

地沟油 (dì gōu yóu)
hogwash oil

Oil retrieved from eatery offal and grease in sewers may be used for individual purposes. But illegal peddlers sometimes sell it as edible oil, causing grave concern among consumers. A city in Zhejiang Province recently raided an edible oil plant and seized 16,500 kilograms of hogwash oil.

地下钱庄 (dì xià qián zhuāng)
illegal private bank

This term means underground banks dealing in illegal money transactions, including exchange, loans and money laundering. China has busted seven illegal private banks this year and seized 44 suspects, including a Singaporean who handled more than 5 billion yuan (US$640 million) in funds in Shanghai.

第一桶金 (dì yī tǒng jīn)
the first bucket of gold

Tons of articles have been published in the press discussing how people make their first fortune and use it to invest in their business.

点击纹 (diǎn jī wén)
clickprint

This is another Chinese translation of the English word "clickprint," which is defined as a unique pattern of Web-surfing behavior based on actions such as the number of pages viewed per session, the number of minutes spent on each Web page, or the time or day of the week the page is visited.

电电车 (diàn diàn chē)
BC trolley bus

Equipped with lithium battery and capacitor, the new environment-friendly electric bus has been introduced into Shanghai recently. It can run for a day with a single recharge and doesn't produce emissions.

电老鼠 (diàn lǎo shǔ)
electricity rat

Those who steal electricity are called electricity rats. In the summer some residents and business owners steal electricity by tampering with their meters. They avoid paying high electricity tariffs by lowering the meter readings significantly.

电脑脸 (diàn nǎo liǎn)
computer face

Despite its many positive attributes, the Internet does change people's lifestyle. After spending hours in front of a computer every day, people gradually look haggard, expressionless, dour and numb to real life and other people. They all have a "computer face."

电眼 (diàn yǎn)
electrifying eyes

Youngsters in China these days use the expression to refer to the beautiful eyes of either a female or a male that are said to send a shiver down the spine of the attracted beholder, like an electric current.

电子标签 (diàn zǐ biāo qiān)
RFID tags

Shanghai has planned to develop Radio Frequency Identification (RFID) tags during the 11th Five-Year Plan period (2006–2010) as one of its goals in boosting the fast-growing IT industry.

电子狗 (diàn zǐ gǒu)
radar detector

Some motorists have illegally installed the "electronic dog," as the Chinese term literally translates, on their vehicles to detect police radars and cameras. The device is designed to help drivers evade traffic monitoring and possibly traffic rule-breaking penalties.

碟托 (dié tuō)
album shill

These shills usually post their opinions or comments on online bulletin boards about a newly-released album to earn money from the record company. They will either be hired to boast about a certain record or attack records issued by rival firms.

丁宠家庭 (dīng chǒng jiā tíng)
pets-only DINK family

This term refers to DINK (double incomes no kids) and "pets-only" families. Such families prefer to have pets rather than children.

丁狗族 (dīng gǒu zú)
DIDK

Some young couples in China's large cities prefer to raise a pet dog instead of having a baby these days. DIDK, double income, dog for kid, is based on the word DINK (double income, no kid).

钉子户 (dīng zǐ hù)
holdout homeowner

The term, literally "nail household," is first used to describe home owners who block new development projects by refusing to move as they look for better terms or compensation from the developers. Now it is also used for anyone who holds out against certain policies or arrangements.

顶风 (dǐng fēng)
storm confronting

The Chinese phrase literally means "against the wind." However, it often refers to the violation of a freshly enforced law or regulation. *Dingfeng* literally means against the wind. Chinese people tend to refer to a newly launched drive to crack down on a malpractice as a storm, like the recent ban on TV commercials promoting weight loss, breast augmentation and medical equipment.

定心丸 (dìng xīn wán)
heart–soothing pill

People tend to take pills to calm the overly fast heartbeat caused by anxiety, concern, worry or extreme uncertainty. The Chinese term for such a pill is also used to describe reassuring advice, a plan, proposal or solution that helps to restore one's confidence.

动车组 (dòng chē zǔ)
bullet train

Bullet trains, with bullet-shaped locomotives, are designed based on aerodynamic theories, allowing the train to run at a high speed. China launched its first batch of homemade bullet trains on April 18, 2007, which can run at 200 kilometers per hour.

冻卵胎儿 (dòng luǎn tāi ér)
snowflake baby

This term refers to an infant born from a frozen embryo. China's first snowflake baby was born in Beijing in April, 2006. US President George W. Bush has banned the use of frozen embryos in scientific research.

动漫 (dòng màn)
manga

The animated cartoons for theater, film, DVD, flash and so on have spread from Japan to the whole world.

冻薪 (dòng xīn)
salary freeze

Due to the ongoing global recession, many companies have been forced to cut their budgets in different ways. Some have sacked employees to save costs while others have imposed salary freezes for the coming year.

兜圈子 (dōu quān zi)
beat around the bush

The Chinese term literally means "walking or running in a circle." It is often used to mean someone acts in a beating–around–the–bush way.

豆腐渣 (dòu fu zhā)
jerry-built (project)

In Chinese, the term literally means made of residue left by processing soybean curd. It is an equivalent to "jerry-built" in English. Such projects in China often involve corrupt business people or officials.

豆腐帐 (dòu fu zhàng)
tofu ledger

The term was used to describe account books made by tofu street sellers who wrote down each sale clearly and counted all the costs and profits at the end of each month. But now it refers to detailed accounts of personal expenditure. Many white-collar workers today love to jot down and share their everyday spending record on the Internet.

都市粗犷男 (dū shì cū guǎng nán)
ubersexual

This is a Chinese translation of the English word ubersexual. It refers to a male who is similar to a metrosexual but displays a bit more traditional manly qualities such as confidence, strength and style.

毒舌派 (dú shé pài)
sharp tongues

The term refers to those judges of some televised singing contests in China who have become bitter and mean in criticizing the contestants. Quite a number of people find such pungent words not only discouraging but also humiliating.

毒枭 (dú xiāo)
drug lord

Liu Zhaohua, an alleged drug lord, went on trial for masterminding the production of more than 18 tons of methamphetamines on June 26, 2006, the International Anti-Drug Day, in Guangzhou, while five major narcotics dealers were executed on the same day.

读奏会 (dú zòu huì)
reading-musical concert

The term refers to a concert that consists of episodes of both reading and musical performances. The term's pronunciation in Chinese is the same as "solo concert" but with the word "solo" replaced by "reading."

堵单 (dǔ dān)
stocks trading jam

The term refers to difficulties in placing orders with brokerages to trade certain securities. It happens quite often these days as millions of new stock investors keep swarming into the market and brokerages' outdated systems fail to cope with the sudden surge in trading volume.

短信诈骗分子 (duǎn xìn zhà piàn fèn zǐ)
SMS scammer

The Public Security Ministry recently disclosed a few shocking cases of criminals using cell-phone short messages to cheat people out of money. Officials say now you can call police for help if you receive such fraudulent messages on your cell-phone.

断背婚姻 (duàn bèi hūn yīn)
Brokeback marriage

Borrowing the name from Ang Lee's movie *Brokeback Mountain*. This term means a current or former marriage in which one partner is gay or has had a gay affair.

断供 (duàn gòng)
mortgage default

The word emerged as housing prices in several Chinese cities started to fall. Many house-owners have refused to continue to pay their mortgages as the value of their property is shrinking.

断腕 (duàn wàn)
desperate act to survive

This term derives from a Chinese idiom describing a heroic man amputating his own hand after being bitten by a deadly poisonous snake. It now refers to anyone who makes a courageous decision to survive a difficult or death-or-life situation by making a major sacrifice.

钝感力 (dùn gǎn lì)
power of insensitivity

It is the ability to face up to setbacks and failures by playing down the painful sting they actually inflict on the sufferer. It comes from the namesake novel by Japanese author Junichi Watanabe.

对台戏 (duì tái xì)
rival show, challenge

The Chinese term means to put up a show next to an existing show to compete for an audience. It can also be used to describe a person or organization taking actions to challenge their rivals.

多宝鱼 (duō bǎo yú)
turbot

The discovery of residue of antibiotics that are believed to be carcinogenic has triggered a nationwide suspension of sales of the popular dish fish.

E

恶搞 (è gǎo)
kuso

The term refers to the online popular fad of turning a famous song, movie or other artwork into a parody that offends some people but amuses others. It is a Japanese word.

二房东 (èr fáng dōng)
second–hand landlord

The phrase means people who rent an apartment from the owner and then lease to other tenants to make money from the price difference. Many property management companies are complaining that some "second–hand landlords" divide apartments into smaller units to rent to more tenants.

二奶 (èr nǎi)
kept mistress

This Chinese term was used in the past to refer to the number two of a man's wives. But today, it is widely used to call a kept mistress who has an ongoing extramarital sexual relationship with a man. She is usually financially supported by the man.

二手短信 (èr shǒu duǎn xìn)
second-hand SMS

It refers to mobile phone messages received from, and sent to, others. There are many such messages of greeting in circulation during holiday seasons. Using them displays a lack of originality, and even sincerity, as they are never your own.

二维码 (èr wéi mǎ)
QR Code

A QR Code is a matrix code invented by Japanese corporation Denso-Wave in 1994. The QR is derived from "Quick Response." Camera mobile phone users with code-reading software can scan the image of the QR Code and be re-linked to a Website that this code represents.

F

发嗲 (fā diǎ)
act endearingly

In Shanghai dialect, not only a young woman but also a man can employ endearment to attract attention or invite sympathy.

发福 (fā fú)
grow stout

Chinese believe that middle-aged people putting on some weight is a sign of well-being. The Chinese character "fu" means felicity, and the term "fafu" is a propitious saying of gaining weight.

发烧友 (fā shāo yǒu)
aficionado, buff

The Chinese term translates literally a "feverish friend." When the world's greatest rock band, the Rolling Stones, played their first Chinese mainland concert in Shanghai, hundreds of "feverish" rock fans shaved up for the event.

发泄餐厅 (fā xiè cān tīng)
anger–venting restaurant

This refers to a special restaurant in Nanjing, which is perfect for anyone wanting to let off steam. It allows diners to smash anything in the restaurant, ranging from dishes and bowls to acoustic equipment, as long as they are willing to pay for the damages.

发小 (fà xiǎo)
friend since childhood

In the Beijing dialect, this term refers to a friend since one's childhood.

翻台面 (fān tái miàn)
clear the table

Many restaurants limit dining hours on the New Year's Eve or busy holiday seasons so that each table can be used to serve more than one group of diners at a meal time. After a table of customers finishes dining,

waiters or waitresses will clear the table to attend to
the next batch of customers.

返聘 (fǎn pìn)
returnment
The term means inviting retired employees to return
to the workforce, a phenomenon of an ageing society
where fewer people are contributing to an occupational
pension.

返券黄牛 (fǎn quàn huáng niú)
shopping coupon scalper
Some shopping malls give coupons to customers as
discounts during promotions. If customers don't want
to use the coupons, scalpers profit by selling or buying them.

反式脂肪 (fǎn shì zhī fáng)
trans fat
Trans fat, also known as trans fatty acid, is made
through the chemical process of hydrogenation of oils.
It has been making headlines as consumers become

aware that the artery-clogging fat is lurking in many food products, including fried fast food.

反水 (fǎn shuǐ)
rebel, betray

It refers to anyone who rebels against the authority or turns his or her back on a friend in an unexpected manner.

反星族 (fǎn xīng zú)
anti-fan

Every coin has two sides. When there are fans, there are anti-fans. The term anti-fan refers to anyone who passionately dislikes a celebrity or other well-known person or entity.

饭搭子 (fàn dā zi)
meal pal

This term refers to office workers who lunch together. Many white-collar workers are seeking lunch pals via the Internet to share high prices as well as the delicious dishes in nearby restaurants.

范跑跑 (fàn pǎo pǎo)
Run Run Fan

Chinese online users have nicknamed teacher Fan Meizhong as Run Run Fan after he fled his classroom, leaving behind all his students, when an 8.0–magnitude earthquake hit Sichuan Province on May 12 2008. He has been widely criticized as being selfish and unethical. In comparison, some other teachers sacrificed their own lives in protecting and saving their students during the devastating earthquake.

饭泡粥 (fàn pào zhōu)
chatterbox, gasbag

This is the name of a favorite breakfast food for Shanghainese, made of rice cooked in water. If you prefer it softer, you cook the rice in the water for a longer time, creating a lot of bubbles. Now, it's used as a nickname for anyone who's excessively talkative.

房虫 (fáng chóng)
house bug

People who buy apartments as an investment rather than accommodation are referred to as house bugs, or house investors. They are blamed on China's mainland for helping drive up the prices of newly developed houses beyond the means of urbanites with average incomes. The central government's policy to control the property market deals a heavy blow to the house bugs.

放单飞 (fàng dān fēi)
fly solo

This term is often used to describe the situation where a team or band is dissolved and each member begins to work individually. It may also be used to mean giving a unique treatment to a single group of people out of a specific social sector.

放倒钩 (fàng dào gōu)
booby trap

A "reverse hook," as the Chinese term means, is dangerous for unsuspicious prey, because it's easy to swallow, but hard to spit out. In a recent case in the city, an official pretended to be a hitchhiker and offered driver a 10-yuan bill as a thank-you token at the end of the ride. But when the driver took the money, the official flashed his ID and pressed charges against the driver for "illegal carpooling."

放鸽子 (fàng gē zi)
stand up, no-show

This Chinese term, flying a pigeon, derives from an old lottery scheme in Shanghai and the fact that the owner who sets free a trained homing pigeon would lose nothing since the bird always knows the way back home. Now, it is frequently used to describe the behavior of standing somebody up, playing no-show or offering empty promises.

放水 (fàng shuǐ)
1.act leniently

It refers to when an authority or superior intentionally bends the rules to let someone off the hook.

2.throw a game, lose on purpose

It usually happens in competitive games. One side loses the game on purpose after reaching a deal with the other side.

放卫星 (fàng wèi xīng)
stand up, no-show

This Chinese term, which literally means "launching a satellite," evolved from the phrase "flying a pigeon." It used to describe making big news during the Cultural

Revolution (1966–1976). But now it is used to describe the behavior of standing somebody up, not showing up or offering an empty promise.

非法集资 (fēi fǎ jí zī)
ponzi scheme

Ponzi scheme, named after its early 20th century inventor Carlo Ponzi, is a form of fraudulent investment scam. In a recent case, a local woman allegedly defrauded more than 50 people, many of them friends and co-workers, out of 7.69 million yuan (US$949,400) involving the sale of pre-paid mobile cards.

非茂型 (fēi mào xíng)
non-mall shopping center

Open-air shopping centers become more popular among customers because of the spacious environment and fresh air. Not like traditional indoor shopping malls, the open-air ones can be surrounded by trees, flowers, even bridges and creeks. Among the 11 shopping centers opened in 2006 in Shanghai, four are non-mall centers.

飞特族 (fēi tè zú)
freeters

It is a combination of English word "free" and the German word "arbeiter," which means worker. It refers to those who work only when they feel they need some money. They have a working time more flexible than freelancers. Usually freeters work part-time in IT, advertising or other media outlets and most of them are well-known in their field of career.

飞线 (fēi xiàn)
jumper wire

Some IT manufacturers prefer to make a shortcut on their circuit boards as a remedy to fix bugs caused by wrong designs. Producers often claim that it is a component. However, users often reject products with jumper wire and consider them as substandard.

飞行特技 (fēi xíng tè jì)
aerobatics

Russian air forces recently staged an airplane acrobatics show in the Zhangjiajie tourist area in central China's Hunan Province. Daredevil though they may be, the air acrobatic team dropped a plan to fly through a hole on the peak of a local mountain because of the dangers and ensuing environment damage.

粉飞客 (fěn fēi kè)
fanfic

An abbreviation for "fan fiction," the term refers to fans who are interested in writing sequels or changing plots of TV series to express their ideas, passions or dissatisfactions.

封口费 (fēng kǒu fèi)
gag fee

This is the price you pay to stop people with inside knowledge from talking about what they know. It can be paid in money, dinners or presents.

孵空调 (fū kōng tiáo)
stay in an air–con place

With the land scorching under the sizzling sun out-side, many love to stay inside all day long with air-conditioning on. However, health experts warn that this could be bad for one's health. From time to time, one should sweat a little and get some fresh air outside. The first character in this Chinese term means "hatching" or "incubating" and the other two mean "air-conditioning." But the first character may also imply "staying put" in a place.

夫妻相 (fū qī xiàng)
husband–wife looks

In the west, people say if a couple live together long enough, the husband and wife tend to resemble each other and even become look-alike. In China, many believe that the marriage will last longer between a man and a woman who share some matching or similar facial features. So, the husband–wife looks are deemed as one of the criteria for looking for one's other half.

福袋 (fú dài)
lucky bag

Lucky bag is a promotion method used by shopping malls. The malls sell several products in a bag, with different combinations, to shoppers at fixed price. The price is lower than the combined retail price of the products in the bag.

伏都娃娃 (fú dū wá wá)
voodoo doll

Voodoo dolls have hit the market in Shanghai as boys and girls buy them in the belief that the dolls can bring good luck to them and bad luck to their enemies. But don't bet all your luck on a small needle that pierces a voodoo doll. Better treat such a doll as fun, not your savior.

福利腐败 (fú lì fǔ bài)
welfare corruption

It refers to special welfare enjoyed by those work in a certain sector (usually a public sector) but denied to others. For example, employees of an electrical power company can enjoy free electricity, while those of a bus company are entitled to take free bus rides.

福娃 (fú wá)
Fu Wa

Fu Wa is the official English name for the five mascots picked for the 2008 Olympics Games in Beijing, though each of the doll-like mascots has its own name, such as Beibei, Jingjing and Yingying. The selection marks the first time that more than three images will share Summer Olympic mascot duty.

腐败捎客 (fǔ bài qián kè)
corruption broker

This phrase mainly refers to lawyers who bribe judges on behalf of their clients. Wu Zhenhan, former president of the Hunan Provincial Higher People's Court, was sentenced to death with a two-year grace period, for taking six million yuan in bribes.

俯卧撑 (fǔ wò chēng)
unfeeling apathy, flimsy excuse

The term literally means "push-up," a form of physical exercise. Now it is used to describe an apathetic attitude or a flimsy excuse. The phrase derives from a news story about a boy who was at the spot of a girl's death. The boy told police when the girl jumped into the river from a bridge, he was doing push-ups a dozen or so meters away, so he saw nothing.

副卡 (fù kǎ)
party partner

He or she accompanies the opposite sex to a party as a lover, sometimes in the sense of an extramarital one which is clear to the other partygoers, though the relationship is not public or acknowledged.

负人 (fù rén)
spend–more–than–earn

The colloquial expression means those who spend far beyond their means and are in debt each month.

负心汉 (fù xīn hàn)
love rat, love cheat

A Website run by a young woman that exposes the private details of men who cheat their girlfriends of not only love, but also property has spawned many follow–up articles. But it has raised concerns about privacy rights and doubt about the credibility of the "sad stories."

复原乳 (fù yuán rǔ)
reconstituted milk

The state standards administrative authority has recently told all dairy producers they must tell customers clearly whether the milk they sell is "reconstituted milk" or "pure fresh milk." Earlier, press reports disclosed that many dairy producers sold the former under the name of the latter in order to cut costs.

G

轧闹猛 (gá nào měng)
follow suit en masse

This popular phrase in Shanghai dialect reflects the fact that many locals love to follow fashion trends, ride the bandwagon, do what most people do and go where most go.

轧山湖 (gǎ shān hú)
chat casually

The colloquial expression in Shanghai dialect means chewing the rag or shooting the breeze. In different localities, there are different terms for chatting idly, such as "*kan da shan*" in Mandarin in northern China and "*bai long men zhen*" in Sichuan Province in southwest China.

干股 (gān gǔ)
gift stocks

The "dry stocks," as the Chinese term translates literally, refer to the shares a company offers to someone as a present. China's Supreme Court has just defined the practice as illegal for government officials.

干货 (gān huò)
substance, real stuff

The term originally means dry cargo or dried food, but it is often figuratively to mean substantial stuff or the essence of things. A person has *ganhuo* if he or she has solid thoughts. A book has *ganhuo* if it is not full of wishy-washy mumbo jumbo.

钢管舞 (gāng guǎn wǔ)
pole dance

It is an irony that some fashion-conscious white-collar women in large Chinese cities like Shanghai and Beijing have taken to pole dancing as a form of exercise in their spare-time while it's often seen as a popular performance at strip clubs in Western countries.

戆大 (gàng dà)
gander

This word is a typical example of Chinglish expressions used in Shanghai dialect. The local pronunciation of the word is quite similar to the English word "gander." The term is used to insult someone's intelligence.

膏方 (gāo fāng)
tonic prescription

This Chinese term means a tonic prescription that has the principal aim of enhancing the immune system functions. Many people, particularly the elderly or the weakly, will seek tonic prescriptions in winter as it is deemed the best season to take tonics.

高考状元 (gāo kǎo zhuàng yuán)
college entrance exam ace

This word means the top scorers in college entrance exams. Such cream of the crop is usually taken away by top universities in the country.

高楼掷物(gāo lóu zhì wù)
killer litter

The term refers to garbage dropped from high buildings. In a mega-city like Shanghai, which is crowded with high-rises, killer litter remains a protracted headache.

高薪跳蚤 (gāo xīn tiào zǎo)
high-salary job hopper

This Chinese term means literally a "high-salary flea." Since a flea can "hop" very "high" considering its small body, the term is actually used to describe highly paid job hoppers.

高压线 (gāo yā xiàn)
top prohibitions

The term means literally a high-voltage line. But it is often used to refer to rules that one should never break because it will prove to be as lethal as touching the high-tension wire.

搞定 (gǎo dìng)
fix something or someone

To *gaoding* someone has almost the same meaning as "fixing" someone. It could mean you have reached a deal with someone, or even have someone deep-sixed. To *gaoding* something also has similar meanings as "fixing" something.

搞脑子 (gǎo nǎo zi)
brain teaser, brain basher

This is a Shanghai colloquial term, meaning something which is difficult to figure out or a problem which takes a lot of brain to solve.

格子店 (gé zi diàn)
pigeonhole shop

A kind of store where cabinet boxes are rented out to different people to sell various types of goods. It has become popular among young people, especially white-collars as they don't have to stay in the store themselves.

个人所得税起征点 (gè rén suǒ dé shuì qǐ zhēng diǎn)
threshold of personal taxable income

China's top legislature recently issued the new threshold for taxable income, 1,600 yuan (US$198) a month, which will be effective from next year. It doubles the previous threshold which was unchanged for more than a decade.

跟风 (gēn fēng)
copycat, follow blindly

A copycat is a person who mimics other people. The word means someone following a trend often in a blind way.

跟帖 (gēn tiě)
follow-up comment

It refers to the comments or articles that are posted as a follow-up to what a thread starter did in a chat room or on BBS.

公费游 (gōng fèi yóu)
junket

The Chinese characteristic of a junket is that it always goes under the name of an official business or assignment. Recently, some senior government officials in Anhui Province were discovered using public funds and false documents to embark on an overseas sightseeing trip.

公司腐败官 (gōng sī fǔ bài guān)
CFO

The term means Corporate Fraud Officer here, not chief financial officer. It is another example of borrowing and twisting the meaning of an existing term.

公寓式仓库 (gōng yù shì cāng kù)
garage condos

The Chinese phrase derives from a US terminology referring to garages located at sites that look like ordinary storage rental facilities, but they come with unusual features, such as heat and air conditioning and clubhouses. They are sold like condominium apartments, where the owner gets title to one unit in a complex of garages. Some buyers use their units to store big boats, fancy cars or collectibles.

孤儿 (gū ér)
office loner

This term, meaning literally "orphan," is often used by young people to refer to an office worker who is isolated, or chooses to be isolated, by others, either because of his or her bad behavior, disputable character or other problems.

孤老 (gū lǎo)
elder orphan

This Chinese term means literally the "lone elder." It refers to an elderly person who has no family or can't obtain any support from his/her family. In China, it also indicates that the elderly person has no pension and is incapable of making a living. This is not a new phenomenon, but the number of them has been increasing quickly as our society ages.

骨感型 (gǔ gǎn xíng)
boney clan

The term means the boney type. Young women who desire a slim figure often follow the example of boney fashion models strutting the catwalk. However, many people see this trend as unhealthy and unattractive.

谷歌文 (gǔ gē wēn)
Googlese text

Scholar Xu Lai coined this term. He uses it to describe written works created by Internet writers who base their text on materials obtained by Googling. Such writers can hardly guarantee the accuracy of their data and frequently risk stepping into plagiarism disputes.

谷歌依赖症 (gǔ gē yī lài zhèng)
discomgooglation

This term refers to the feeling of distress or anxiety at being unable to gain immediate access to information. It's a portmanteau of discombobulate, meaning to confuse or frustrate, and Google. According to a survey, about 44 percent of Internet users in the UK said they were frustrated at being unable to go online and 27 percent said they experienced increased stress levels.

谷歌炸弹 (gǔ gē zhà dàn)
Google bombing

This Chinese translation of the English term means setting up a large number of Web pages with links that point to a specific Website so that the site will appear near the top of a Google search when users enter the link text.

骨灰级 (gǔ huī jí)
guru

Those well-acclaimed masters in a field are referred to by today's youngsters as someone at a *guhui* level. However, caution is suggested when speaking in the face of such a master, if he or she is elderly, as he or she may take offense at the Chinese term, which means bone ashes.

古惑仔 (gǔ huò zǎi)
offbeat boys

The phrase refers to teenagers who pursue an unconventional lifestyle and behavior, including weird hairstyles and clothing and accessories. They also tend to drink alcohol, smoke cigarettes and get into street fights. They account for about 70 percent of juvenile delinquents in big cities across the country.

古墓贴 (gǔ mù tiē)
age-old post

Some Netizens love to update old posts published on BBS several years ago to the front page in order to arouse a new round of discussion. The Chinese term here means literally a post from an ancient tomb.

挂羊头，卖狗肉 (guà yáng tóu, mài gǒu ròu)
bait and switch

The popular Chinese term translates literally "advertising with a sheep's head, but actually selling the dog meat." It is often used to describe the bait-and-switch tactic when someone tries to sell inferior or substandard stuff in the name of quality products.

怪咖 (guài kā)
geek

The slang refers to those intellectuals obsessed with mind games, such as sudoku and crosswords. Although being described as a geek tends to be an insult, the term has recently become a fond nickname, or even a badge of honor.

官府菜 (guān fǔ cài)
official's home cuisine

Most cooks at residences of senior officials in feudal China were able to prepare specialty dishes. The recipes passed down for generations have helped establish some restaurants offering such dishes, like Beijing-based the Tan's Restaurant.

官瘾 (guān yǐn)
lust for official power

Guan in Chinese means "officialdom." *Yin* means "lust." This Chinese term describes many people who lust official power.

灌水 (guàn shuǐ)
flood-blogging

When *guanshui* is used in the context of Internet, it does not mean "irrigation" as in its normal use. Some Web bloggers upload tons of nonsense or neither here nor there trivial in order to earn more online credits but only to be scorned by blog viewers for wasting their time and the server space.

光棍儿节 (guāng gùn er jié)
Singles' Day

Every year at 11:11pm on November 11, fun-seeking male college students will have rowdy parties by screaming out their desire to find a girlfriend and use whatever is available to make big noises. The timing, consisting of eight Arabic number of 1, is deliberately selected to personify many single people. Can you envisage a Single Women's Day?

硅谷新贵 (guī gǔ xīn guì)
IT nouveau riche

The in expression refers to either those high-end IT talent who ride the wave of spending on fashion products and services like spas or those are never tired of undergoing silica gel-based plastic surgeries. The first two words of the Chinese expression mean Silicon Valley while the latter means nouveau riche.

果冻族 (guǒ dòng zú)
jelly clan

It refers to those young Chinese born in the 1980s who are seen as soft and fragile as jelly. They usually have pleasant looks but a weak heart and boast little resistance against pressure.

过劳模 (guò láo mó)
overworked workers, model of models

Those who work far more than eight hours a day, either voluntarily or otherwise, are called a "*guolaomo*," or an overworked worker. Accordingly, they may draw either juice of joy or poison of pain from the long working hours. The term is coined after the word karoshi.

过劳死 (guò láo sǐ)
karoshi

This Chinese term is a direct translation of "death from overwork." The term first appeared in Japan in the late 1980s to describe a new phenomenon of high-ranking business executives dying in their prime years without any previous signs of illness. Now the same thing is happening among middle-aged Chinese businessmen and professionals.

H

哈密瓜 (hā mì guā)
Harry Potter fan

Hami melon, as the Chinese term means, is a special sweet, juicy fruit produced in Hami area of northwestern China's Xinjiang Uygur Autonomous Region. But today in the global craze about the books about a young wizard, it is borrowed to mean Harry Potter fans. Because of the similarity of their pronunciation, the three Chinese characters in this term are used to represent "Harry Potter," "fan" and "muggle."

哈证族 (hā zhèng zú)
certificate maniac

Many job-seeking youngsters, like graduating college students, devote their time to preparing for exams that award an array of certificates proving their language and computer skills in the hope of securing an edge over other applicants in the job market.

" 海带 " (hǎi dài)
"seaweed"

The word, a follow-up to "sea turtle," is used to refer to those Chinese youths who haven't found a job in their home country after they study overseas. The Chinese character *dai* in the phrase sounds the same as another Chinese word meaning "wait" as in waiting for a job.

海根 (hǎi gēn)
back-to-the-root Chinese

Hami melon, as the Chinese term means, is a special sweet, juicy fruit produced in Hami area of northwestern China's Xinjiang Uygur Autonomous Region. But today in the global craze about the books about a young wizard, it is borrowed to mean Harry Potter fans. Because of the similarity of their pronunciation, the three Chinese characters in this term are used to represent "Harry Potter," "fan" and "muggle."

" 海龟 " (hǎi guī)
"sea turtle"

People have come to use this term to refer to people who have returned to work on the mainland after completing their education overseas. "Sea turtle" in Chinese is pronounced the same as the abbreviated phrase "returning from overseas."

海姆 (hǎi mǔ)
Ham, amateur radio operator

This is the transliteration of the English word ham, or amateur radio operators. The source of the name ham is not known but it has been around almost from the beginning of amateur radio in the early 1900s. The name amateur has nothing to do with skill or knowledge but rather implies that ham radio cannot be used for commercial purposes.

海鸥 (hǎi ōu)
globe–trotting businesspeople

Seagull, as this Chinese term means literally, describes some Chinese people who have an overseas education background and frequently take business trips to foreign countries. They are likened to seagulls flying over the sea all the time.

海泡 (hǎi pào)
overseas–lingering grads

Some Chinese students stay much longer than necessary in a foreign country after finishing their study because they lack confidence to find a good job in their home country. The expression plays on the Chinese word "泡," which can mean either bubble, froth or, as a verb, to linger.

海漂 (hǎi piāo)
Shanghai drifters

Young white–collar workers from other provinces who pursue their career dreams in Shanghai are called Shanghai drifters. They live in a rented residence and change jobs frequently.

海投 (hǎi tóu)
resume flooding

As the job market turns grim, job hunters send their resumes in large numbers randomly to various companies in the hope of scooping a few chances of being interviewed.

海豚音 (hǎi tún yīn)
dolphin-vocal-sounding

Zhang Liangying, one of the three winners in Super Girl contest in 2005, is known for her dolphin-vocal-sounding, a special singing technique. Mariah Carey is said to be the one who can use the technique best.

海选 (hǎi xuǎn)
competitive election

The Chinese term is very vivid, which means selection from a sea of candidates. It also means that anyone can vote for his or her favorite candidate. As Super Girl Contest, the Chinese version of the American Idol, gets popular, "*haixuan*" has become a buzzword again.

寒促 (hán cù)
winter promotion

It refers to sales promotions initiated by IT firms during the winter vacation or Chinese Lunar New Year holiday seasons.

含金量 (hán jīn liàng)
true value

The phrase literally means gold content, but in daily use, it is often employed to describe the true value of almost everything, ranging from an academic paper to a business project.

韩流 (hán liú)
Hallyu or Korean fever

Hallyu is a Korean word meaning the boom in Korean pop culture among Chinese, Japanese and Southeast Asians. It also sounds the same as the Chinese term "cold snap."

汗语 (hàn yǔ)
chat-room jargon

This is a team coined to refer to those buzzwords common in online chat rooms or articles but completely incomprehensible to those who read only mainstream publications. It plays on the phrase "汉语" meaning Mandarin, which is pronounced exactly the same way. "*Han*" in the former means sweat, reminding one of the characters sweating in an exaggeratedly profuse way when they are frightened, embarrassed, shocked or frustrated.

行头 (háng tou)
gear

Some children in middle schools vie with each other to wear fashionable clothing and accessories. The equipment needed for a sport or professional activity, like roller skating, mountain climbing or firefighting, is also referred to as *hangtou*.

好人卡 (hǎo rén kǎ)
nice guy card

This is today's answer to the "dear John letter" of the 1940s. A girl may turn down an admirer by saying "You are a nice guy, but I'm sorry we are not suitable." So if a guy says he has "received a nice guy card" that means he has been rejected. The "card" has also developed into "nice guy pop culture." Some designers are creating "nice guy" cards and sell them online.

合同能源管理 (hé tóng néng yuán guǎn lǐ)
EMC (energy management contract)

It refers to an energy conservation service sold to companies to improve energy usage.

贺岁片 (hè suì piān)
New Year movie

Hesuipian, which refers to movies celebrating the New Year, often premiere between Christmas and Spring Festival. Most such movies are comedies and often have an all-star cast. Chinese director Feng Xiao-gang is the most famous in this genre. Total box office revenue of movies he directed has exceeded 1 billion yuan (US$146.26 million) with his latest hit "If You Are the One."

黑暗料理街 (hēi àn liào lǐ jiē)
night food street

The term, which literally means "preparing food in the dark" in Chinese, refers to small food stalls set up along streets, particularly at night. Despite the fact that these vendors sometimes are unlicensed, some people regard eating at them as a way to enjoy local delicacies.

黑吃黑 (hēi chī hēi)
just desserts, shark eat shark

The Chinese term is usually used to describe a situation where a member of the underworld is wiped out by another. It can also be used to depict the "dog-eat-dog," "wolf-eat-wolf" or "shark-eat-shark" clashes in any organization that is deemed in a negative way.

黑广告 (hēi guǎng gào)
illegal ad poster

The city's Huangpu District authority is planning to launch a campaign to stop illegal advertising posters in the Bund area, which are mostly phone numbers about fake medicines and other illicit businesses. Some people also call the posters "psoriasis" because of their ugly appearance.

黑屏 (hēi píng)
black screen

It's the latest Microsoft scheme to fight piracy. It replaces the screen wallpaper of a computer using pirated Microsoft Windows and Office software with a black screen every hour when the computer is turned on.

黑手机 (hēi shǒu jī)
unlicensed cell phone

Unlicensed cell phones in China are a big family which includes millions of smuggled and refurbished cell phones. Illegal vendors or producers make huge profits by selling them, which are assembled based on used fittings or those smuggled from overseas. Many domestic mobile phone makers are complaining these cheaper unlicensed cell phones have eaten away their market shares.

黑嘴 (hēi zuǐ)
black mouth

It refers to all people who brag shamelessly in order to cheat. For example, stock commentators who brag they can always beat the market are dubbed "black mouth."

轰趴 (hōng pā)
home party

The Chinese term is a vivid translation based on the pronunciation of the English term. The Chinese term, however, has a far more interesting connotation. It means at a home party, you can have fun until you physically collapse.

红色旅游 (hóng sè lǚ yóu)
Red Tour

Backed by local governments, many travel agencies around the country have been organizing tours to sites related to the Chinese revolution in the last century, hence the new phrase. The venue of the first meeting of the Communist Party of China in Shanghai near Xintiandi, has become a major Red Tour attraction.

红色炸弹 (hóng sè zhà dàn)
red bomb

As the price tag of wedding gift money keeps rising, more people worry when they receive wedding party invitation cards, usually wrapped in a fancy red envelope. They call such red envelopes "red bombs." They may easily cost you several hundred to several thousand yuan depending on how close you are to the bride or bridegroom.

红头文件 (hóng tóu wén jiàn)
red-head document

This is a colloquial Chinese term for formal, official documents. They invariably bear the full name of the government or the government department that issues the document and the name is always printed in red on the top of the document's front page.

红眼航班 (hóng yǎn háng bān)
red-eye flight

China's aviation regulator has lifted the ban on red-eye flights, which refers to flights departing from 12:00am to 6:00am, as passengers deplaning from such flights tend to have blood-shot and bleary eyes because of sleep deprivation.

呼死你 (hū sǐ nǐ)
phone number jamming

"Call you to death," as this term means literally, refers to a special tactic employed by some city inspectors to deal with illegal ads posted on walls or telecomm poles. The city inspectors record and type the phone numbers on those ads into a special voice mail system, which automatically call those numbers around the clock. As a result, those phones have to be turned off or suspended.

湖绿 (hú lǜ)
fraud

"Green Lake," as the term means in Chinese, refers to cooked-up story. It originated in a popular bbs where someone identified as "green Lake" claimed he had watched a dramatic film which didn't exist. Now his online name is synonymous with falsehood or fiction in online conversation.

护犊族 (hù dú zú)
pampering parents

While people tend to criticize young people living off their parents and becoming NEET (Not in Employment, Education or Training), they have also begun to blame the phenomenon on those parents (and sometimes grandparents as well) who mollycoddle their grown-up children.

护考 (hù kǎo)
exam escort

The practice repeats itself during the annual college entrance exam every year. Parents accompany their children to the exam venue and wait anxiously outside till the exam is over. They make reservation for lunch at nearby restaurants and some even rent a room to make sure that their children eat and rest well during the break between two exams.

花样美男 (huā yàng měi nán)
androgynous man

The on-going "my Heroes" TV talent contest brings us a fresh notion of androgynous beauty. This term refers to those boys or men who are nice looking (especially with feminine features), who wear long hair and act with less-masculine characters.

滑头 (huá tóu)
slippery fellow, Teflon character

If someone has a "slippery head," nothing can be stuck on it. Chinese use this term to describe persons to whom criticism does not seem to stick or people who are cunning and sneaky.

话题广告 (huà tí guǎng gào)
paid blog comment

It is a way of advertising a product among the bloggers.

Paid bloggers will post comments on certain products produced by the hiring company.

话题女王 (huà tí nǚ wáng)
hot topic queen

This term refers to women who always live in the spotlight of mass media and many people just love to watch and listen to their love stories or scandals. The typical representative of such women is Paris Hilton.

环球语 (huán qiú yǔ)
globish

This term means "Global English." It's a simplified version of the English language, using a vocabulary of about 1,500 most common words. It is used by people whose mother tongue is not English.

换房旅游 (huàn fáng lǚ yóu)
home-swap travel

Exchange houses with the people who want to spend their vacation in your city and have a cheap holiday in theirs. This way you can collect great local insider tips and the money saved on hotels can be used to extend your stay abroad.

换客 (huàn kè)
barter clan

Some young Chinese netizens love to trade their belongings by posting information on the Internet, but few have been successful, either because those who post an offer live too far away for a face-to-face exchange of goods or those who post a matching offer never show up for the trade.

换脸手术 (huàn liǎn shǒu shù)
face transplant

Six candidates for China's first face transplant are waiting in a hospital in Jiangsu Province. The ideal patient will be chosen within two months and will be given surgery for free. The youngest candidate is a 6-year-old girl.

换软档 (huàn ruǎn dàng)
relent, soften

The Chinese colloquial expression is commonly used to describe someone yielding to influence or pressure, particularly, after he's been hit in a soft spot.

黄段子 (huáng duàn zi)
dirty joke, juicy episode

Chinese tend to call anything porn "yellow," such as "yellow book," "yellow movie" and "yellow picture." Here, the Chinese term *huangduanzi* means literally "yellow episode," which now often appears in chat rooms, cell phone short message and at dinner tables.

黄昏恋 (huáng hūn liàn)
sunset love, December heartbeat

While Chinese youths are traditionally compared to the rising sun, the elderly are associated with the setting sun. Hence, a romance involving two seniors is often called *huanghunlian*, which literally means "love at dusk."

黄梅天 (huáng méi tiān)
plum rain season

The season is a 20-odd-day period of wet weather that occurs each year around the time when plum gets ripe. It usually begins in mid-June and ends in early July in areas along the middle and lower reaches of the Yangtze River.

黄鱼车 (huáng yú chē)
flatbed tricycle

"Croaker vehicle," as this term translates literally, is the name of a flatbed tricycle for transporting goods and sometimes, passengers. Some say it got its name because it was previously used to vend croakers, but others say it's because such vehicles can ply the narrow alleys in the city like the fish.

灰镜头 (huī jìng tóu)
seamy picture

Hui means dirt or grey in Chinese, and *jingtou* means lens. Pictures taken when the lens is blurred with dirt are considered a disaster. People now use this expression to refer to anything that causes the majority of the public to frown.

灰水 (huī shuǐ)
gray water

Waste water discharged from the washing machine, kitchen and other sources. It can be re-used as it is not so heavily polluted.

回炉 (huí lú)
retraining, further education

It originally means to melt down scrap metal or recook bakery to get it reprocessed or achieve a better flavor. These days, the term refers to people who re-enroll into an educational institute to improve oneself to get better prepared for competition in the fierce job market.

会虫 (huì chóng)
conference parasite

This term refers to those who pretend to be participants in meetings by holding fake name cards or other people's invitations for free food or souvenirs offered by meeting organizers. The term sounds similar to "bellyworm" in Chinese.

婚奴 (hūn nú)
wedding slave

In some Chinese cities, especially large ones like Shanghai, quite a few young couples run into deep debt after throwing a luxurious wedding well beyond their means. So, after the marriage, the newly-weds have to slave away to pay off all the bills.

混搭 (hùn dā)
mix-match

This term is popular with fashion-conscious youths when they talk about the practice of achieving an original effect by intentionally wearing clothes of drastically different styles, that would cause traditionalists to raise their eyebrows.

混枪势 (hùn qiāng shì)
muddle through

In Shanghai dialect, this expression is a form of pidgin that combines the Chinese word, 混 "hun," which means to muddle along, and the transliteration of the English word "chance."

火锅奖 (huǒ guō jiǎng)
hotpot prize

Instead of a jackpot, this term refers to some lottery prizes with a very small value—so small that you can afford only a hotpot meal with each of the prizes.

火腿 (huǒ tuǐ)
HAM, radio amateur

This Chinese term, meaning literally "ham" (the thigh of the hind leg of an animal), is borrowed from English "HAM," referring to radio amateurs. It derives from the amateur radio station operated in the early 1900s in Harvard University by Elbert S. Hyman, Bob Almay and Paggy Murray. H–A–M are the initials of their surnames.

火星贴 (huǒ xīng tiē)
post from Mars

It refers to posts which are considered very old, have been published online long ago, could be seen everywhere, and are considered out of date by most viewers in a chat room.

火星文 (huǒ xīng wén)
textspeak

Young people nowadays tend to shorten words or use words from different languages, numbers and punctuation signs in their text messages, thus creating a kind of new language, or the Martian language, as this Chinese term literally means. Examples: *lol* = laughing out loud; *b4* = before; *RU cmin out 2nite?* = Are you coming out tonight?; *Cul8rk?* = See you later, okay?

I

i- 世代 (i shì dài)
i-generation

This term, translated from English, refers to people who have grown up with Internet and digital technology, and for whom online plays a pivotal role in shaping their opinions and aspirations, and how they approach their personal relationships and professional lives.

J

机车 (jī chē)
slow, picky, pesky
The term, meaning literally "train engine," is often used in Taiwan to describe someone who's either slow, picky or pesky. It may also be used to describe something annoying or vulgar.

鸡冻 (jī dòng)
excited
The term means literally "chicken jelly." Since its pronunciation is the same as the word "excited" in Chinese, it is usually used in online context to replace the conventional phrase.

缉毒犬 (jī dú quǎn)
sniffer dog, drug detector dog
Local airports have employed some sniffer dogs not only to help detect drugs, but also to uncover any

products that could be related to the spreading of avian flu virus. It's reported that the canine squad has been working very effectively.

积分族 (jī fēn zú)
bonus–point clan

It refers to those urban people, especially the young people, who spare no effort in paying by credit card instead of cash to earn more bonus points from the card issuer.

基民 (jī mín)
fund investor

The past year has seen more and more citizens in Shanghai investing in the fund market instead of the stock market, giving the bigger profits.

机械舞 (jī xiè wǔ)
popping dance

A type of dance similar to break dance, which features tightening and flexing of the muscles, just like a robot.

鸡仔文学 (jī zǎi wén xué)
Chick lit

This Chinese phrase is a translation of the English term "Chick lit," which refers to the kind of fiction created for young women, particularly single, working women in their twenties and thirties.

急婚族 (jí hūn zú)
hasty marriage clan

It refers to those who marry hastily, mostly under the pressure from work or family or after waiting too long to find the right partner.

急痞 (jí pǐ)
zippies

Zippies are those who are fond of higher living standard, brave to show ambition and grasping every possible opportunity. They are willing to do anything that may give them chance to succeed.

即开即兑彩票 (jì kāi jì duì cái piào)
scratch lottery ticket, instant lottery ticket

This term refers to the scratch-off tickets of lottery. Lotteries, long frowned upon as a form of gambling in China, gained legitimacy in 1984 with the launch of the first state-sponsored offering.

家包 (jiā bāo)
homesourcing

This term refers to a hot trend of hiring people who work from their home. For instance, independent contractors employ people to handle customer service calls from their home, which saves time and money for both employers and employees.

加急时代 (jiā jí shí dài)
a hurry-up era

People in large cities always seem on a rush to meet all kinds of deadlines and demands because of market competition and high-paced work environment.

假跳 (jiǎ tiào)
tell a lie

The term, literally meaning "false jump," originally comes from "PK: Police and Killer," a role-playing game popular among white-collar workers and college students. When the "policeman" deliberately mistakes a civilian for the killer, he is "false jumping," or in other words, telling a lie.

架空历史 (jià kōng lì shǐ)
alternate history

Also called virtual history or alternative history. It is a mixture of speculative fiction, science fiction and historical fiction. Usually set in a fantasy world whose history has diverged from the actual world, alternate history literature asks the question, "What if history had developed differently?"

减副 (jiǎn fù)
reduce deputy posts

The Chinese term has the same pronunciation as that for "reducing burden," but it replaces the Chinese word for "burden" with one that means "deputy posts." In some Chinese cities and townships there are simply too many deputies allocated to a single administrative chief. Such bureaucratic padding has drawn wide criticism and actions to reduce the number of such deputies.

减压经济 (jiǎn yā jīng jì)
pressure-alleviation economy

This term is used to denote an economic sector that involves services that ease the pressure of everyday life, such as karaoke bars, sewing clubs, mood food, spas and weekend farmers.

见光死 (jiàn guāng sǐ)
killer light

The Chinese phrase means someone dies by being exposed to the light. Now, it is used to describe the unfortunate outcome of the first date between two people who have fallen in love after chatting on the Internet and/or on the phone without ever seeing each other in person. The romantic bubble often bursts when the two meet in real life as delusion is dispelled by reality.

贱男 (jiàn nán)
a loose man

It refers to promiscuous men, especially those in the entertainment industry, who hop from bed to bed or who never treat love or marriage seriously.

江湖义气 (jiāng hú yì qì)
communalism, brotherly loyalty

Jianghu, the first two characters in this term, means literally "rivers and lakes." But it often refers to a world beyond the establishment, a world of the outlaws or just the big wide world where vagrants with skills or ambitions or both seek fortune and fame. Credit and loyalty are deemed as the two pillars of the non-mainstream society.

降价死 (jiàng jià sǐ)
price-cut death

It refers to the phenomenon that once the government orders a price cut on a certain drug, the manufacturers will immediately stop making the product and then repackage the "dead" drug under a new name to sell for higher prices.

酱油男 (jiàng yóu nán)
soybean sauce man

Taken up by Internet users after a man responded during an interview that he was just out to buy soybean sauce and didn't care about the question. "I'm just out for soybean sauce" has become a euphemism for "it's none of my business."

茭白 (jiāo bái)
worried white-collar

The Chinese term, originally the name of the wild rice shoot (a vegetable), is now used to describe a worried white-collar worker plagued by the fear of being laid off amid the global economic recession. The first character of this Chinese term sounds like the word "worried" and the second here stands for "white collar."

交通拥挤费 (jiāo tōng yōng jǐ fèi)
congestion charge

The city is considering to introduce a congestion charging scheme similar to the one imposed in central London to help cut traffic jams during rush hours. If enacted, the scheme will charge drivers when they enter a certain downtown area during a given period of time.

嚼吧 (jiáo bā)
chewing gum club

It is reported that in some big Chinese cities like Beijing and Guangzhou, a chewing gum producer has set up a room and offers free products to office workers complaining of high pressure, either from work or life, in high-end office complexes.

脚底抹油 (jiǎo dǐ mǒ yóu)
cut and run

The term literally means "to apply oil to the soles of one's feet" so one can retreat expeditiously. It is commonly used to describe someone who leaves the scene suddenly to avoid difficulties or trouble.

搅局 (jiǎo jú)
spoil the party

Action movie star Jackie Chan recently created a disturbance in real life by exchanging insults with the audience when he appeared as a guest singer at Taiwan singer-songwriter Jonathan Lee's concert in Hong Kong.

较真 (jiào zhēn)
extremely rigid, uncompromising

This term describes a person who believes in downright exactness and is always prepared to go to great lengths to get things right.

街拍 (jiē pāi)
street snapshot

Many shutterbugs these days upload the pictures they have taken on the street onto the Internet to share with others.

阶梯计价 (jiē tī jì jià)
volumetric pricing

Volumetric pricing is a tiered pricing system used in Tokyo and 12 Chinese cities including Nanjing and Shenzhen. It charges heavy users higher fees compared to light users, which encourages conservation.

姐弟恋 (jiě dì liàn)
cradle snatcher

"Sister-younger brother love," as this term means literally, refers to a woman's romance with a much younger male partner. It is not only reflected in the couple's appearance, but also in their roles in this relationship.

节日综合症 (jié rì zōng hé zhèng)
post-holiday blues

After a long holiday, many people tend to feel fatigued, listless, absent-minded, and out of step with the fast rhythm of the workplaces. It usually takes a couple of days for people to readjust before they are back to the normal workday pace.

节约型社会 (jié yuē xíng shè huì)
conservation-oriented society

Due to urgent short supplies of energy, raw materials and other resources, the Chinese government has been urging the whole nation to go all out in building a more conservation-oriented society in order to pursue sustainable social-economic development.

解套 (jiě tào)
cut paper losses, extricate oneself

This term, originally meaning getting out of the noose, is often used in the stock market to refer to a situation where the investors cut the paper losses when the value of their share rebound to the original prices or higher. It may also mean someone extricates himself from entanglement of difficulty.

借壳上市 (jiè ké shàng shì)
backdoor listing

Backdoor listing, also called reserve takeover, refers to attempts by a non-listed company to acquire a publicly traded firm to go public. A slew of Chinese mainland brokers are now seeking to conduct backdoor issues as they fail to meet regulatory requirement of posting profit for three consecutive years or they want to find a faster and cheaper way to be listed.

金龟婿 (jīn guī xù)
rich husband

In ancient China's Tang dynasty (AD 618–AD 907), only certain high-ranking officials coul carry the "golden turtle pouch" as a rank symbol, hence a "golden turtle husband" as the Chinese term literally translates, was used to refer to a husband with a very high social status. But today, it only means a rich husband.

金牌学历 (jīn pái xué lì)
gold-medal education

This term doesn't mean an education that is worthy of a "gold medal." It refers to the free education offered by some universities to attract sport stars who have won gold medals.

金融海啸 (jīn róng hǎi xiào)
financial tsunami

People often use the expression to describe, if not exaggerate, the current financial crisis that is looming large across the world.

紧急避孕药 (jǐn jí bì yùn yào)
morning-after pill

It's a medical method to help prevent unwanted pregnancies following unprotected sex or failed contraception. The Shanghai Family Planning Instruction

Institute will cooperate with the Shanghai Pharmaceutical Association to train pharmacists and clerks at 1,000 drugstores on the proper use of the morning-after pill.

京骂 (jīng mà)
Beijing expletive

This term has become well known in China after some spectators being heard shouting loudly expletives in typical Beijing dialect and tone during live TV broadcasts of some sports games, particularly soccer games, in the capital.

井喷 (jǐng pēn)
blowout, cough up

A recent gas blowout happened in southwestern China's Chongqing and forced more than 14,000 people to evacuate from their homes while firemen and specialists tried several times to cap the leaking gas well.

净足风暴 (jìng zú fēng bào)
football purging storm

The term refers to the judicial intervention in the

match–fixing scandal centered on Juventus, one of Italy's football giants. The first half of the Chinese phrase means "make the football clean."

救场 (jiù chǎng)
emergency stand–in

When an actor is not available for a performance that cannot be rescheduled, another may offer or be invited to stand in. In daily life, a person can rush to the help of another one who is unexpectedly unavailable for a job by acting as a substitute.

居家养老 (jū jiā yǎng lǎo)
home–based care for the aged

To cope with a quickly–aging society and the sharp shortage of facilities for the elderly, Shanghai has been advocating the so–called *jujia yanglao*, or home–based care for the aged. The city has adopted a number of measures, such as improving the community–based services and introducing schemes of providing cared and emergency aid to senior citizens who are living alone by pairing them with other families.

剧透狂 (jù tòu kuáng)
spoiler junkie

This term refers to people who are addicted to learning plots of TV or movies before watching them. But they may accidentally tell their friends about the ending of the movie, thus taking away all the excitement and suspense.

巨无霸 (jù wú bà)
superjumbo

The Airbus A380 visited China's three major cities, Shanghai, Beijing and Guangzhou, as part of its 17-day worldwide show of the Toulouse-based plane maker's technology. An object or a large-scale business establishment is also referred to as a superjumbo.

掘博 (jué bó)
Blog digging

Blogs have been becoming an increasingly popular method for people to record their lives and share their experience with others. Many people also like to read others' blogs. They dig into archives to learn more about the blog owner.

掘客 (jué kè)
(digg) digger

This is a new kind of Website on which Netizens can publish any story. If other Internet users like the story, they can click on it, and the more clicks a story receives, the more likely it will move to the Website's front page.

K

卡爆族 (kǎ bào zú)
overspending cardholder

It refers to usually young people who always spend not only above their monthly incomes but also beyond the quota of their credit card.

卡布奇诺经济 (kǎ bù qí nuò jīng jì)
cappuccino economy

This Chinese term, translated from the English phrase "cappuccino economy," refers to an economy that displays frenzied growth or activity in one sector while showing only steady growth or activity in other sectors.

卡奴 (kǎ nú)
card slave

Along with the popular use of credit cards in some large cities in China, some card users, especially youngsters with large shopping addictions and small salaries, gradually become credit card slaves, because they borrow from one credit card to pay off debts on another credit card. Due to their meager salaries, they always live on the edge of bankruptcy.

卡神 (kǎ shén)
card manipulator

The term is the opposite to "card slave," people who borrow from one credit card to pay off debts on another credit card and live on the edge of bankruptcy. The card veterans can make the most of their credit cards or membership cards to earn points and benefits.

卡娃 (kǎ wá)
card kid

It's a new term referring to teenagers who disseminate all kinds of advertising cards, such as discounted air tickets, to pedestrians or bicyclists in streets or other public places. They have become a public nuisance as they literally harass people while distributing the cards. Last year, Shanghai street cleaners collected 24 tons of such cards.

开光 (kāi guāng)
consecrate, deify, bless

Usually, newly-built temples and Buddha statues need to be consecrated before they are put into service. In order to seek good luck, nowadays people request monks to help consecrate or bless a great variety of personal articles, ranging from talismans and ornaments to cell-phone numbers.

开瓶费 (kāi píng fèi)
bottle-opening fees

Restaurants always charge bottle-opening fees if customers bring drinks by themselves. Many people complain that the rule is a "despot term" and refuse to pay the fee.

看野眼 (kàn yě yǎn)
look around distractedly

This is a colloquial term in Shanghai dialect meaning looking around aimlessly, absent-mindedly and distractedly. Traffic authorities say many road accidents have resulted from motorists looking away from the road in an absent-minded or distracted manner.

考托 (kǎo tuō)
exam scalper

This term refers to people who register online to possess exam qualifications and then sell registration numbers to real exam goers.

考碗族 (kǎo wǎn zú)
civil servant test sitter

Against the backdrop of the global recession, more young Chinese people nowadays look for a secure job as a civil servant, usually nicknamed as the "gold rice bowl." So, they all sit for the examinations designed for winning such jobs. Chinese traditionally refer to a stable job as an "iron rice bowl."

靠谱 (kào pǔ)
proper, relevant

The word is frequently used these days to mean an idea, act, plan or policy that is considered acceptable by the public or tradition.

可爱的上海人 (kě ài de shàng hǎi rén)
amiable Shanghainese

The term "lovable Shanghainese" derives from a city government campaign urging locals to be friendly and helpful to out-of-towners and to behave in a civilized way.

啃老族 (kěn lǎo zú)
NEET

It stands for Not in Employment, Education or Training. It refers to some young people who do not work but live off their parents.

啃椅族 (kěn yǐ zú)
seat squatter

This term refers to people who occupy a chair or table in fast-food restaurants and spend several hours there reading books, surfing on the Internet or chatting with friends regardless of other customers' need for a seat.

空窗期 (kōng chuāng qī)
dry spell, available

The "open-window period," as the Chinese term translates verbatim, refers to a respite when a person is not dating anyone after a break-up.

空降兵 (kōng jiàng bīng)
parachute manager

This term originally means a parachute soldier. Like someone dropping from the sky, it now often refers to new managers brought in from outside an enterprise. However, it's quite common for such managers to face big orientation problems and incapability in bringing about expected results.

空军 (kōng jūn)
no-house class, no-housers

This term is used in online chat rooms and BBS by urban residents, especially those youngsters who own no house. The Chinese term literally means air force in English.

空头捐赠 (kōng tóu juān zèng)
fictitious donation

Many companies and individuals have made generous donations to the victims of the magnitude 8 earthquake that hit China's Sichuan Province on May 12 2008. But some firms have failed to make good on their donation pledges.

空心汤团 (kōng xīn tāng tuán)
empty promise

There is a typical Shanghai snack called "*tangtuan*" or glutinous rice flour dumplings with fillings served in soup. In the case you are given an empty promise, the Shanghainese tend to say that you are served with "*kongxin tangtuan*" or dumplings without fillings.

空中飞人 (kōng zhōng fēi rén)
frequent flyer

This Chinese term, "man flying in the sky," is sometimes used to refer to trapeze artists. But here it refers to frequent plane travelers.

恐婚族 (kǒng hūn zú)
marriage–shy clan

The term is used to describe some young people who are extremely afraid of making the commitment to get married. The same people are totally at ease with pursuing dating relationships.

控盐勺 (kòng yán sháo)
salt–control spoon

Shanghai government has decided to give out 6 million salt–control spoons free to local families in order to help control local residents' daily salt intake. Scientists have found that locals are putting too much salt into their food. Surveys found an average resident in Shanghai takes in about 9.90 grams of salt every day, far above the recommended amount of 6 grams.

抠抠族 (kōu kōu zú)
eke–out clan

Some young office workers in large cities like Shanghai who have a meager income have to think of varied ways to save money to pay their mortgages or to cover their wedding costs.

口红效应 (kǒu hóng xiào yìng)
lipstick effects

The term describes the tendency for consumers to purchase small, comforting items such as lipstick rather than large luxury items amid economic downturns. For example, Shanghai United Cinema Lines, the city's leading cinema chain, benefited from lipstick effect by taking more than 495 million yuan (US$72.4 million) in box office receipts last year, a 29-percent increase from 2007. The nation's movie theaters also took in 4.2 billion yuan in 2008, an increase of 888 million yuan from 2007.

口水歌 (kǒu shuǐ gē)
resung song

Some mediocre singers have to sing the hit songs of pop stars or well-known folk songs to attract an audience and build their way to stardom. Such resung songs are also popular with karaoke goers as they are usually within ordinary people's singing capability.

口水战 (kǒu shuǐ zhàn)
saliva war

People these days refer to the endless rounds of

published criticism and counterattacks between two persons or groups as a saliva war.

苦肉计 (kǔ ròu jì)
play pain card, no-pain-no-gain scheme, smoke screen

It was originally a Chinese military strategy where a general was beaten up in public to show he had been purged in order to be placed in the enemy's confidence. These days, people mean it to be a scheme to win eventual success by undergoing hardships or widespread reforms first.

苦手 (kǔ shǒu)
slouch, bungler

The two Chinese characters in this term literally mean "bitter" and "hand." The phrase, originating from the Japanese word "negate," is used to describe a person who is not good at something or is inept in handling a situation.

酷抠族 (kù kōu zú)
cool miser

It is reported that some rich people in Nanjing, Jiangsu Province, have followed a fad of living a simple and frugal life, although they can afford a more costly lifestyle, to save money and other resources.

酷游族 (kù yóu zú)
cool explorer

It means those metropolitan youth who are keen on outdoor exploration during their spare time. It is reported that about 60–70 percent of the cool explorers in Shanghai are females.

快闪暴走族 (kuài shǎn bào zǒu zú)
smart mob

This term is a translation of the English term "smart mob." According to Howard Rheingold, author of the book *Smart Mobs: The Next Social Revolution*, the people who make up smart mobs cooperate in ways never possible before because they carry devices that possess both communication and computing capabilities. The evolving communication technologies will greatly change the way that people organize and share information.

快速时尚 (kuài sù shí shàng)
fast fashion

Also known as high-street fashion, it involves shoppers getting the latest clothes just a few weeks after they first appear on the catwalk and at reasonable prices.

宽粉 (kuān fěn)
super fans

This Chinese term means literally "thick glass noodle." Since glass noodle, which sounds like the English word "fans" in Chinese, has been widely used as a moniker of fans, the "thick" ones naturally become "super" fans.

款爷 (kuǎn yé)
moneybags, fat cat

This term consists of two Chinese characters, namely, "money" and "big shot." So its meaning is self-evident. But it's a slangy term and used often in the northern part of the country.

狂扫族 (kuáng sǎo zú)
crazy shopper

Some shoppers buy whatever is available at a sale only for the cheap prices: the extreme example of impulsive buying.

L

拉风 (lā fēng)
cool, eye-catching

The word, which literally means draw the wind, is believed to have come from a line in a Hong Kong-made movie starring Stephen Chow. Today's trendy people use it to refer to anything that is cool, original, outstanding, posh, or sexy.

垃圾 (lā jī)
rubbish

This term translates literally "garbage" or "trash." But when it is used to refer to people or their behaviors in Shanghai dialect, it means they are despicable, contemptible or disgusting.

拉郎配 (lā láng pèi)
forced match

The expression originally refers to usually illmatched

marriages arranged by matchmakers or parents in ancient China. These days, people use it to describe a forced match or combination of different groups of people or entities, such as some government-orchestrated mergers of companies and banks.

喇叭腔 (lǎ bā qiāng)
bugle, screw up

In Shanghai dialect, when people talk about "bugle tune," they actually mean something's botched up. This is because Shanghai locals believe the bugle tune sounds like saying "going wrong, going wrong" in their parlance.

辣妈 (là mā)
yummy mummy

Compared with people's traditional thoughts of a mother, a yummy mummy usually looks sexy and has an open-minded air. As younger women become mothers, the number of yummy mummies is on the rise.

来电 (lái diàn)
tingle, spark, be electrified

Chinese often say there's an "electric current" flowing between a man and a woman. They may say they feel "a spark." So, if one wants to decline a relationship, he or she might blame the shortage of electricity.

赖床 (lài chuáng)
sleep in, lie in

The expression refers to the habit of some people who spend an unduly longer time in bed, especially on holidays and weekends, enjoying the well-deserved leisure and laziness to compensate for a busy week or work schedule.

赖园族 (lài yuán zú)
park lingerer

The term refers to people who linger in walled parks after it was closed and are not willing to leave. Park rangers need to clean them out from each corner of the park. Lingerers may walk dogs, date with friends or do anything they wish in closed parks, mainly at night.

兰花指 (lán huā zhǐ)
orchid fingers

This refers to a finger sign arranged by touching the tips of one's thumb and middle finger and aiming the pointing finger, ring finger and pinkie of the same hand into the air. The resulting "orchid fingers" are frequently used by actresses in Chinese operas, such as Peking Opera. A man will be considered sissy if he does "orchid fingers."

懒婚族 (lǎn hūn zú)
single-life clan

It refers to those who have a decent and well-paying job and live a comfortable life but are reluctant to get married.

劳务费 (láo wù fèi)
service fee, labor fee

The expression usually refers to the money paid for a service, odd job or specific project, but sometimes it is used as a disguise for kickbacks or bribes.

老大难 (lǎo dà nán)
nagging problem, nuptially challenged

This is a very common Chinese term as everyone could face some "old, big problems" (if translated verbatim). However, it is also frequently used to call bachelors or spinsters who have passed the best marrying age and now find it difficult to find a desirable person to marry.

老法师 (lǎo fǎ shī)
senior specialist, elder cognoscente

This term is often used humorously to refer to a person who is both senior in age and expert in a certain aspect of life or knowledge.

老克勒 (lǎo kè lè)
class, cognoscente

This is a well-known Chinglish term in the Shanghai dialect, which derived from the English word "class" of "classy" in the 1930s and 1940s. The Chinese term was used to describe the "high-class" Shanghai gentlemen who lived a Western-style life in the city. Now, it also has a connotation of being around a lot and knowing all the answers.

老赖 (lǎo lài)
deadbeat

The city recently sent 80 diehard defaulters to jail. They were all debtors who had the money but refused to pay court-ordered debts. *Laolai* is a derogatory term in Chinese.

老娘舅 (lǎo niáng jiù)
avuncular arbitrator

In Shanghai dialect, the Chinese term, an uncle on the mother's side, is often used to depict an avuncular person who plays the role of an unofficial arbitrator for neighborhood or trivial disputes.

老婆本 (lǎo pó běn)
wedding savings

Many Chinese men save money when they begin working and the savings will be used to buy a house, home appliances and other important articles in order to marry a woman.

老人老办法 (lǎo rén lǎo bàn fǎ)
grandfather policy

It's a common practice in China to follow the principle of "old rules for old staff" as this Chinese term literally translates. But actually, it means an exemption based on circumstances existing prior to the adoption of a new policy so that those who were recruited earlier won't be affected by the new policy.

老鼠仓 (lǎo shǔ cāng)
rat trading

The term has recently come into the spotlight as some mainland brokers were believed to have made illegal profits by conducting so-called "rat trading" or a kind of scalping scheme in the stock market by cheating their clients.

老爷车 (lǎo yé chē)
jalopy, antique car

The Chinese word refers to both an old, dilapidated vehicle and those classic automobiles well worth collection. Shanghai was the destination for an antique car race beginning in Hamburg.

老油条 (lǎo yóu tiáo)
sly person, misconduct repeater

The term refers to wily people, especially those who stay in an environment long enough to be able to take advantage of existing loopholes for their own benefit or goof off in the work place. It may also be used to describe those who commit multiple misdemeanors.

老字号 (lǎo zì hào)
time-honored business

Chinese traditionally believe in shops or industrial establishments that have survived decades or centuries of competition from their rivals.

乐触族 (lè chù zú)
LOTAF

The term stands for "lifestyle of touch and fun." It refers to people who are interested in and enjoy using touch screen digital devices, such as iTouch and iPhone.

乐活族 (lè huó zú)
LOHAS

It is the acronym of "life style of health and sustainability," referring to a group of people who are optimistic, understanding, caring about environment and health, and doing good and as well as feeling good. This concept originated in Britain in the middle of last century.

雷词 (léi cí)
shocking word

The Chinese term, which literally means "thunder word," refers to newly-coined shocking and outrageous words or phrases. They are extremely popular in online chat rooms and blogs.

蕾丝边 (léi sī biān)
lesbian

The Chinese term is basically a transliteration of the English word "lesbian," but with a much more vivid image as it literally means the fancy laces of women's stockings, petticoats, pajamas and bras.

雷招 (léi zhāo)
outrageous measure

The Chinese term literally means a "shocking measure." It refers to any shocking, extraordinary measures, such as unexpected sales promotion schemes offered to buyers visiting housing exhibitions.

冷暴力 (lěng bào lì)
cold violence

This term describes a type of family problem as one party in a marriage constantly refuses to communicate with the other party or uses various means to cause mental pain to the latter. Unlike physical violence which is detectable when it develops to a certain degree, the cold violence is mostly in the dark, but it has become a major reason for family breakup in many places.

冷笑话 (lěng xiào huà)
bad joke

Some bad jokes are very popular in many online forums these days. Many are not funny, but someone may laugh at it for no apparent reason.

利好 (lì hǎo)
bullish news, favorable news

It refers to any news, like a positive earnings report or favorable policies by the government, which drives up the price of a company's shares.

立军令状 (lì jūn lìng zhuàng)
make a sworn pledge

This is a very popular Chinese term that derives from a centuries-old practice in the military when someone makes a written pledge to carry out a mission, the failure of which will subject him to military punishment. Now, people use it to mean making a sworn pledge to accomplish something.

立升 (lì shēng)
high-heeled clout

The word in Shanghai dialect originally describes the volume of a container. A person with "volume" now means a high-heeled investor or a person with clout.

联体别墅 (lián tǐ bié shù)
townhouse

China's recent ban on approving land for villas has pushed some developers to seek loopholes in the new rules by building townhouses.

连体婴儿 (lián tǐ yīng ér)
conjoined twin babies

A pair of conjoined twins who were in a Shanghai hospital awaiting separation surgery have died, and their parents have donated their bodies to medical research.

练摊 (liàn tān)
vending business

The Chinese term, used more frequently in northern China, refers to the vending business people conduct either on roadsides or on the Internet. Several Websites, such as www.taobao.com, have become very popular with owners of small vending businesses.

两地分居 (liǎng dì fēn jū)
long-distance marriage

Because of a rigid residence registration system, it was quite common in China about two decades ago that a married couple lived in two locations far apart. This situation is similar to the long-distance relationships in Western countries, but the Chinese term is used almost exclusively for married couples.

拎包党 (līn bāo dǎng)
bag grabbers

The term refers to thieves who grab someone's bag and run away when he or she fails to guard it tightly in a public place. Such robbers usually act with accomplices and often employ bicycles, motorbikes or other getaway means.

临时抱佛脚 (lín shí bào fó jiǎo)
make hasty, last-minute efforts

The Chinese term means literally to hold the Buddha's feet just before the need for a blessing. It is often used to describe someone making hasty, last-minute efforts to tackle some problems, which usually prove to be too little and too late.

零绯闻 (líng fēi wén)
gossip–free

While some mediocre showbiz artists, especially actresses, tend to fabricate love stories and have them published to attract attention, others just walk all the way to stardom and even to an accomplished retirement without any such gossip.

零号 (líng hào)
size zero

This term originally means a US size in women's clothing, which is equivalent to size 4 in UK. But now it's also used to describe a small, fashion model–like body.

零口供 (líng kǒu gòng)
zero confession

For a long time after new China was founded, court authorities refrained from convicting a defendant who didn't confess to a crime he or she was charged with. However, in recent years, when they feel the evidence is sufficient, they will go ahead with the ruling without the defendant's confession.

零人格 (líng rén gé)
zero integrity

This term refers to someone who has no integrity. It first appeared in the Hong Kong media and has led to another term called "negative integrity," meaning worse than "no integrity."

零容忍 (líng róng rěn)
zero tolerance

This Chinese term is actually a translation of the English term "zero tolerance." It means extreme intolerance of bad or anti-social behaviors.

零团费 (líng tuán fèi)
zero inclusive fee

This term refers to a sales promotion widely used by travel agencies, which attract tourists to attend their package tour by paying only a small amount of money, which usually includes air tickets, admission to scenic sites and some other fees. However, those travel agencies will earn profits from tourists by guiding them to buy some worthless but very expensive souvenirs and jewelry in local stores.

灵异事件 (líng yì shì jiàn)
paranormal event

This term refers to ghost reports, monster sightings, psychic experiences and other mysteries of the unexplained. China Central Television recently broadcast a series of programs on how to debunk fake paranormal events, which caused a lot of complaints because of the scary scenes.

领便当 (lǐng biàn dāng)
die, game over

During the shooting of a movie, a helper can get a meal box after he finishes his job. So, fetching a meal box, as this term means literally in Chinese, indicates that the play is over for the helper and he is no longer needed. It may also mean the death of somebody or the end of something.

另类 (lìng lèi)
offbeat

This term has become popular as people tend to use it to describe anyone or anything that ranges from avant-garde to unconventional or weird.

撩菜 (liáo cài)
entice a woman

It is slang used these days at nightclubs and cafes to refer to a man trying to engage the attention of a woman and make advances to her.

撩火腿 (liáo huǒ tuǐ)
go gigolo-ing

It refers to a man who is looking to link up with a rich woman for both a romantic relationship and to entice continuing financial support from her.

疗伤系 (liáo shāng xì)
soother, balm

First used to refer to a style of song featured in a Japanese album that is characterized by soothing melodies, the expression now refers to any cultural product that can set your mind at rest. It is also used to refer to a kind of person that is gentle and endearing.

撩汤 (liáo tāng)
entice a man

The female version of seducing the opposite sex at an entertainment venue.

溜冰 (liū bīng)
taking ice

Since "ice" is widely used as the nickname for crystal methamphetamine hydrochloride, a powerful synthetic stimulant drug, people in China use *liubing*, which means "ice skating," to describe the abuse of the drug.

榴莲族 (liú lián zú)
durian clan

It is a fad in China these days to label different kind of people with the name of fruits, such as the strawberry clan (good looking but easily perishable) and the coconut clan (being unafraid of pressure). Now, the durian clan refers to people who are just the opposite of the strawberry clan.

流氓软件 (liú máng ruǎn jiàn)
malicious software

Malicious software refers to viruses, trojans, worms, spyware, and similar threats, which may provide you some unnecessary information or functions or steal useful data from your computer. Most of them are hard to remove.

留守儿童 (liú shǒu ér tóng)
cold-nest kids

A man buying the virginity of nearly 20 teenage girls in Henan Province whose parents were away doing migrant work has again raised public concern for kids who live in a home short of parental warmth and proper education.

留爪 (liú zhuǎ)
leave a mark

The term literally means "leaving a claw mark" in Chinese. Now the phrase is becoming popular among online users when referring to making an online posting in BBS communities.

龙凤胎 (lóng fèng tāi)
boy–girl twins

It is deemed extremely auspicious among Chinese for a woman to give birth to boy–girl twins or the "dragon–phoenix twins" as the Chinese term literally means. An Anhui woman delivered quadruplets, two boys and two girls, in Shanghai last week.

笼户 (lóng hù)
cage dweller

To earn more rent, some owners have partitioned their apartments into many very small rooms before renting them out. Some young people, particularly those who are single and new to the city, prefer to live in such "cages" before they decide to buy a home. They are called "cage dwellers."

楼主 (lóu zhǔ)
thread starter

The person whose article or comment on the BBS or online chat room triggered off discussions and arguments on a specific topic is often referred to as a thread starter. As his or her article or comment appears at the very top of a string of remarks, a thread starter is therefore nicknamed as *louzhu* (chief of the building). The following debaters are called dwellers of the second-floor, third-floor, etc, according to the appearance sequence of their comment.

路怒 (lù nù)
road rage

Poor traffic conditions and endless traffic congestions in crowded cities and on expressways could trigger violent behavior or road rage by a driver as he acts out his frustrations. The road rage, in turn, may lead to accidents or incidents on roadways.

驴友 (lǘ yǒu)
tour pals

The literal translation, "donkey pal," sounds the same as the Chinese word for travel. It refers to the increasing number of backpackers who team up for budget tours after making the arrangements over the Internet rather than through a travel agency.

驴子 (lǘ zi)
heavy-pack traveler

This Chinese phrase means literally donkey, a working animal. It is used here to describe those travel buffs who are equipped with professional backpack gear, such as a sleeping bag, tent and water cask. The name implies that they travel with heavy packs, just like a donkey carrying a large piece of cargo.

旅游购物狂 (lǚ yóu gòu wù kuáng)
transumer

Chinese tourists are now well-known for their shopping sprees overseas at souvenir stores, shopping malls and brand name boutiques. Transumer, a newly-coined English word that blends "transient" with "consumer," is the best name for those Chinese tourists.

绿标 (lǜ biāo)
green sticker, emission decal

The Shanghai government has recently issued a green sticker to every car that meets the emission standards and banned the rest from using the elevated roads during the day time. The new rule, however, has unintentionally helped spawn a fly-by-night business of selling fakes to those whose vehicle has slim chance of passing an emission test.

绿电 (lǜ diàn)
green electricity

Power suppliers in Shanghai have kicked off this year's sales campaign for "green electricity," as part of efforts to promote wind and solar energy to curb pollution and meet growing power demand.

绿婚 (lǜ hūn)
green marriage

It refers to the kind of marriage where the sense of environment protection is best embedded: The invitation letter is printed on recyclable paper, and the newly weds and wedding attendants ride a bicycle or walk to the party where they enjoy "green" food and drinks.

绿领 (lǜ lǐng)
green-collar

A green-collar has the stamina of a blue-collar, education of a white-collar and wealth of a gold-collar. They pursue a healthy and environment-friendly lifestyle, like shutting cell phones after work to ensure enough free time, never eating without heeding nutrition, spending weekends traveling out-of-town whenever they can, and the signature one—always taking a trash bag to clean up pet's waste.

绿帽子 (lǜ mào zi)
green hat

In China, you never give a man and particularly a married man a green cap or hat. He may very well take it as an insult, because it's the symbol of a cuckold in the Chinese culture. So, when you say a man's wearing a green hat, you actually call him a cuckold.

绿游 (lǜ yóu)
green tour

A term used these days to classify those people who prefer a tour operator and a hotel that provide environment protection information, refuse to eat or buy anything made of protected species and refrain from littering and using detergents.

乱入 (luàn rù)
please come in, pop in

The term originally means to enter a place without permission. But as slang widely used in BBS, it now means to invite others to come in freely. For a Netizen, who needs others to answer his or her questions or just read his or her post in a BBS, the person may use this term in the headline to attract attention.

螺蛳壳 (luó sī ké)
tiny space, small apartment

The Chinese term literally means a "snail shell," but it is used figuratively to describe a tiny space or a very small apartment.

裸奔 (luǒ bēn)
streaking

It is non-sexual act of taking off one's clothes and

running naked or with very little clothes on through a public place. The most public form of streaking is running naked before huge crowds at sporting events.

裸捐 (luǒ juān)
all-out donation

The word, which literally means "naked donation," appeared in the online world after the founder of Microsoft, Bill Gates, said he will donate all his property—worth a total of US$58 billion—to charity work after his retirement. So, if someone donates all of his or her assets to a cause, he/she is making a "naked donation."

裸考 (luǒ kǎo)
naked exam

This is word-for-word translation of the newly invented Chinese term. It does not mean that one takes a test with nothing on. It means a "pure test," in which no one can get any special treatment, such as winning additional points because of one's other talents or performance. In the past, student who have artistic or athletic gifts, were often given extra points on their academic exams.

裸聊 (luǒ liáo)
nude web–cam session

Police in Jiangsu Province have caught a hacker who snuck into a couple's nude web–cam session, and took stills of the wife and e–mailed them to the couple "for fun."

裸体做官 (luǒ tǐ zuò guān)
corrupt officials ready to flee

The word, which literally means "naked corrupt official" in Chinese, refers to officials who have managed to move all their family members to foreign countries so that they can flee immediately if their crimes are uncovered.

裸替 (luǒ tì)
nude stand–in

Nude stand–in refers to people who substitute big stars in movies for nudity shots. A nude stand–in for movie star Zhang Ziyi in "The Banquet" recently popped up in the spotlight of the media by telling her own stories and career.

裸投 (luǒ tóu)
unbagged trash

Some residents have begun to dump their trash "naked," as this Chinese term translates literally, after the
government banned free plastic bags offered by shops
or supermarkets earlier this year. Formerly, many people used old plastic bags as garbage bags.

裸装食品 (luǒ zhuāng shí pǐn)
unpackaged food product

"Naked" food, as this Chinese term translates literally, refers to unpackaged food products, particularly
frozen or processed. City authorities have recently
banned local food stores and supermarkets from selling "naked food," believing they are more susceptible
to contamination during handling and transport.

落差婚 (luò chā hūn)
mismarriage, left-handed marriage

It refers to a marriage in which the husband and wife
are a breed apart in terms of wealth, age, height,
social status and other relevant aspects.

M

M一代 (M yī dài)
multitasking generation

This is a term created by the US-based Time magazine. It refers to the young people who indulge themselves in Internet games, iTunes, MySpace, MSN and other online activities, sometimes simultaneously.

麻袋帮 (má dài bāng)
big-bag shopper

The term refers to people who usually appear at big discount sales of brand name consumer products, such as clothes, shoes and cosmetics. They buy rapaciously and carry away their purchase in big bags they have brought with them. But just hours later, these goods will appear in online shops with their prices redoubled.

马甲 (mǎ jiá)
online alias

The Chinese term literally means waistcoat. Now, it's also used to describe fake names a Net surfer uses for chat-room discussions or as a camouflage to support himself or herself by posting articles under fake names.

骂山门 (mà shān mén)
make a fuss about nothing

The dialect commonly used in Shanghai and neighboring areas is believed to have originated from making a scene without any good reason to show anger at monks at the gate of a temple, who are generally too tolerant to offend others.

麦霸 (mài bà)
microphone monopolist

This term is used by frequent patrons to a karaoke bar to describe a friend who dominates the singing party by keeping the microphone to himself or herself.

麦工 (mài gōng)
McJob

Labor authorities in the city are investigating several fast food giants on allegations of paying McJobs less than the minimum wage. Merriam—Webster Dictionary has recently adopted this slang and defined it as a low—paying job that requires little skill and provides little opportunity for advancement, to the dismay of the fast—food giant McDonald's.

麦时尚 (mài shí shàng)
McFashion

Hennes & Mauritz (H&M), the largest clothing and cosmetics retailer in Sweden, opened its first store in Shanghai in 2007. Offering designer—looking clothes for a small budget, fashion brands like H&M and Zara are described as McFashion, as fashion has begun to resemble fast food: fast and cheap.

馒头门 (mán tóu mén)
Bungate

Hu Ge, a Chinese young man made an Internet parody, entitled "The killing over a bun" to satirized "The promise," one of the most expensive films ever made in China by Chen Kaige, a famous Chinese film director. Chen threatened to sue Hu over copyright violation. Now, Bungate has become a hotly-debated controversy in China.

慢城 (màn chéng)
slow-paced town

This Chinese term sounds the same as the translation of the name of the British city Manchester, but it actually means a town or city with a slow-paced lifestyle.

冒泡 (mào pào)
bubbling

The term refers to those who issue a post in a BBS after keeping silent for a long time, just like a bubble quickly rises and then disappears.

美丽垃圾 (měi lì lā jī)
beautiful garbage

The phrase refers to the over-extravagant gift packing made of materials such as metal, glass, silk or even rosewood. Despite the beautiful look, people usually throw it away after unpacking, causing a big waste.

闷骚 (mēn sāo)
surprise package

The term refers to people who look plain, cold or even dull outside, but inside they are volatile, charismatic, hot and sexy. It may also be used to describe a person's duplicitous personality, but mostly in the eulogistic sense.

门槛精 (mén kǎn jīng)
pettily shrewd

This is a colloquial expression in Shanghai and its neighboring areas to refer to a person who is good at scheming to gain petty advantages and sophisticated in trivial issues.

门萨 (mén sà)
Mensa

It is a club that pools those with high IQ scores for the common interest of working out solutions to rare and weird questions. The word in Latin means a table, and the club borrows it to mean a round-table society, where the members span a wide variety of jobs, from delivery man to lawyer.

迷卡 (mí kǎ)
mini card

It refers to portable digital input cards with handwriting functions, usually in the size of a name card. It proves to be a welcome alternative to keying text into phones or other electronic devices.

密码疲劳症 (mì mǎ pí láo zhèng)
password fatigue

Ever-growing involvement in the Internet life often brings forward a syndrome where people are required to remember an excessive number of passwords. Such stress may cause people to take risks by lowering their guard against online identity fraud.

蜜运 (mì yùn)
serious dating

When a man and a woman are dating seriously and

it is likely leading to a marriage, young people tend to say the duo are in "*miyun*" or struck by "honey luck." This Chinese term is coined after the term "honeymoon" because of their causality and their similar pronunciation in Chinese.

免费续杯 (miǎn fèi xù bēi)
free top-up

As a popular service in China and around the world, free top-up is a useful sales promotion for restaurants, bars, cafe or tea houses to attract more customers.

免提听筒 (miǎn tí tīng tǒng)
chatterbox

It literally means the hands-free telephone receiver. In daily talks, youngsters use it to describe those super-talkative guys who just keep on talking as if to themselves and don't even bother to wait for any response from listeners.

面霸 (miàn bà)
interview buster

Some young people are always on the hunt for better jobs even though they already have one or got other offers. So, they take endless interviews at different places. The Chinese term was borrowed from a well-known instant noodle brand because the two Chinese characters, "face" and "buster," have some implication of such a phenomenon.

民间食神 (mín jiān shí shén)
popular foodie

The term refers to ordinary gastronomes who are fond of sharing their experiences on Websites and making comments on restaurants that they have visited. They have been attracting a growing number of followers and beginning to influence the culinary trends among the public and even in the catering industry.

民心工程 (mín xīn gōng chéng)
heart-winning project

It refers to a project which benefits ordinary people, such as building affordable housing for low-income earners.

名分 (míng fèn)
birthright, given status

The word usually refers to the status a mistress seeks from her lover or an illegitimate child seeks from her biological father. These days, people often use it to mean an official status that a person or organization deserves.

名片鼠 (míng piàn shǔ)
name–card mouse

It is a new type of computer mouse in the shape of a name card holder. It is lightweight and extremely portable.

名人博客 (míng rén bó kè)
celeblog

Many celebrities nowadays have set up their own blogs to reach out to their fans or to further extend their influence. This new term, however, means either a blog written by a celebrity or a blog devoted to a particular celebrity or to celebrity news and gossip.

明日黄花 (míng rì huáng huā)
déclassé

The Chinese term literally means "tomorrow's chrysanthemum." It came from an ancient Chinese poem, in which the poet asked his guest to stay to appreciate the flower right then, because it would wither the next day. This term can be used to refer to people or things that have become out of fashion and of little value.

名嘴 (míng zuǐ)
popular TV presenter

The word literally translates as "famous mouth," a catchword for those well-acclaimed television anchorpersons.

摸石头过河 (mō shí tóu guò hé)
improvise by trial-and-error

The Chinese phrase translates literally "crossing a river by feeling the stones at the bottom of it." Now it is often used to describe the approach of moving ahead in an uncharted territory by groping along and improvising.

摸我 (mō wǒ)
MSN me

The first letter of MSN sounds like the Chinese word "*mo*" or touch. So, MSN users in China often use the term "touch me" to ask someone else to keep him or her posted via the instant online message tools.

摩客 (mó kè)
mook

It is a combination of magazine and book, which is regularly published and can be subscribed to. This form of publication, which first appeared in Japan, has become quite popular among young people.

末端时尚 (mò duān shí shàng)
tip-top fashion

It refers to trendy hairstyling and manicures pursued by many young women. As the makeover involves the woman's head hair and fingernails and toes, it is hence called "tip-top" fashion.

拇指族 (mǔ zhǐ zú)
oyayubizoku, clan of the thumbs

The word came from Japan first. It refers to people who are skilled at using their thumbs to manipulate objects such as mobile phone keys, small joysticks, and notebook computer pointers. Now more and more Chinese young people have joined the clan of the thumbs as they use SMS as their major communication channel.

N

奶油妈妈 (nǎi yǒu mā ma)
milky mom

The term refers to mothers who, after the prescribed four-month maternity leave, have to go back to work but keep feeding their babies with their own milk. So, they have to find time and proper places to collect their milk during work hours and then bring the milk home after work. Since thousands of babies have recently fallen sick after taking some tainted milk powder products, the "milky mom" has become a healthy trend.

男人妆 (nán rén zhuāng)
unisex makeup

Some women make themselves up in a way that is unisex instead of purely feminine.

脑体倒挂 (nǎo tǐ dào guà)
limbs before brains

The phrase refers to the phenomenon that some talent-intensive jobs such as researchers are paid less than labor-intensive ones such as meter readers when industries are not market-oriented.

脑子进水 (nǎo zi jìn shuǐ)
bubble brain

If water is injected into the brain, as this Chinese term reads verbatim, it won't be able to work very well. This term is commonly used these days to mean someone who is being stupid or confused.

闹洞房 (nào dòng fáng)
bridal chamber pranks

It's Chinese tradition that guests crowd into the bridal chamber to tease the newly-wed couple after the wedding banquet. Anything goes here and sometimes it turns into a rather rowdy gathering that lasts late into the night.

内定 (nèi dìng)
predetermination

It usually refers to the process of making decisions on choosing candidates or leaders to certain positions in government departments, companies, work units or organizations before the official announcement or going through some prescribed formalities.

内功 (nèi gōng)
inner power

The term originally referred to the rare power a kungfu master accumulated in the inner organs, such as control of breathing to enhance the impact of a punch. These days, people often use it to describe an organization's competitiveness and efficiency resulting from its internal system and innovation.

内鬼 (nèi guǐ)
inner culprit

The Chinese term means literally "inner ghost." It refers to the perpetrators, spies or any kind of wrongdoers inside an organization. Because they work from inside, it's usually rather difficult to discover their moves.

内紧外松 (nèi jǐn wài sōng)
floating duck tactic

This translation is based on the English term of "floating duck syndrome," which describes a situation where a duck paddles frantically underneath in order to keep its body calmly floating on the water. In China, however, people don't see it as a syndrome, but a tactic to hide one's efforts in speeding up his work or in controlling damages underneath a calm and relaxed appearance.

(你) 太有才了！(nǐ tài yǒu cái le)
You're so gifted!

This was the jape repeatedly cited by a female comedian in a show at this year's Spring Festival television gala, now a *sine qua non* of the Chinese New Year celebration. Since then it has become so popular, and it is widely used in daily conversations to flatter someone for his/her smarts.

娘娘腔 (niáng niáng qiāng)
sissy, pansy

The English phrase originally refers to a weak man or a homosexual. People in Shanghai use the Chinese phrase to describe boys or men who talk or behave in an effeminate way.

鸟人族 (niǎo rén zú)
bird people

In colloquial Chinese, this is not a term for creatures in science fiction, fantasy fiction or mythology. Instead, it refers to people who move their home frequently, on an average of two to three times a year, in a city like Shanghai. Their purposes are to find novel living environments, new lifestyles or to meet particular personal needs, such as sleeping in an absolutely quiet room.

牛皮癣 (niú pí xuǎn)
nagging problem, eyesore ads

The term for a skin disease, psoriasis, is often used to describe a prolonged nagging problem. It may also be used to depict the eyesore ads, such as illicit trashy ads posted or printed on walls, telecomm poles, door steps or even pavements, which are very difficult to get rid of.

NONO族 (NoNo zú)
NONO clan

The word came from best-seller Naomi Klein's book "No Logo" in 2002. It refers to young people who pursue a pure and environmentally friendly life that refuses any luxurious products. Though well-off, they despise all the famous brands but prefer goods with strong individual styles.

农家乐 (nóng jiā lè)
farmer's home inn

During the weeklong golden holidays, people often cannot find hotels in popular sites, so some farmers will lend their houses to tourists, which are cheaper than normal hotels. Tourists can also eat with the farmer's family and do farmer chores for fun.

女猪 (nǚ zhū)
heroine, female protagonist

"Pig" and "protagonist" have similar pronunciations in Chinese except for their tones, so do not mistake the term for "female pig" next time you see it online — it is actually a trendy way of saying heroine among the literature fans on the Internet.

O

OBS 女人 (OBS nǚ rén)
OBS woman

Already over 30, they still keep the lifestyle of a young girl. It doesn't matter whether they are still single or married. They always walk down the street in girlish outfits and spend money on products originally targeting a younger generation. OBS stands for the Japanese word obasan, meaning "aunt" or "adult woman in general."

呕像 (ǒu xiàng)
disgusting icon

The term sounds the same as another Chinese term *ouxiang* which literally means an idol. These days anyone who has managed to gain fame, through negative, nasty means, is called a disgusting icon.

P

爬梯 (pá tī)
party

Chinese Netizens these days use this term, which literally means "ladder-climbing," as a substitute expression for "party" as the Chinese expression sounds just like the English word.

拍车门 (pāi chē mén)
door-tapping robbery

Police said a new form of robbery is on the rise in big cities, where a lot of cars are often trapped in traffic jams every day. Drivers might meet a friendly person knocking on their front doors when they stop at a red light or park beside the road. The person will ask the driver some ordinary questions. When drivers are concentrating on talking to the person, accomplice will open the car's backdoor and snatch any valuables in the car.

拍书族 (pāi shū zú)
bookstore shutterbugs

This Chinese term refers to people who take pictures of contents of new books in bookshops for their own use. Some even post such materials on the Internet to be shared by others. Now, some local bookstore owners are preparing to sue those people for "book theft."

拍砖 (pāi zhuān)
knock, pick apart

The term, which literally means "smacking with a brick" in Chinese, is now widely used among Chinese Internet users when they strongly criticize someone's idea or act.

排 (pái)
agreed

At online chat rooms, Netizens use this Chinese word, meaning literally to queue or line up, to express their agreement to an opinion. It roughly means to get into the queue or stand in the same line as others.

排客 (pái kè)
paid queuer

This term refers to people who are paid to stand in a queue for others. This is a new service, particularly in the booming real estate market. In some cities, people have to queue up for a long time to buy an apartment. To save time, some buyers hire others, usually migrants from rural areas, to stand in the line for them.

∏型人才 (π xíng rén cái)
∏-type talent

It is a kind of person that has good command of two fields of professional skills as well as having expertise in management and administration. The two professional skills are the two vertical strokes while the administrative expertise is the horizontal one.

盘点 (pán diǎn)
elaboration, rundown

It originally means stock counting. But now the term is widely used in the media to mean to cover a certain topic in an exhaustive way or to summarize the overall developments.

抛抛族 (pāo pāo zú)
public litters

Some spectators at concerts or sports games have adopted the annoying and disruptive habit of littering, extending to even throwing things on stage and court. This behavior tarnishes the image of their city.

抛绣球 (pāo xiù qiú)
throw an embroidered ball

Throwing embroidered satin balls is often seen in games played by young people of minority nationalities in China. Also, a young woman may throw an embroidered ball to a young man at a ceremony as a way to choose a husband. Now it can also be used to mean an opportunity offered by someone or some organization.

跑酷 (pǎo kù)
parkour

Parkour is a new sport inspired by human movement. It focuses on uninterrupted, efficient forward motion over, under, around and through obstacles especially in an urban environment. The goal of parkour is to adapt one's movement to any given obstacle.

跑龙套 (pǎo lóng tào)
walk-on

The term originally means a minor role in a theatrical production which usually has no speaking lines. But in daily conversations, it refers to anyone who only plays a bit role such as a utility man or a general handyman in any event, project or business.

泡菜 (pào cài)
kimchi

A possible origin of kimchi or Korean spicy traditional pickled vegetables was in ancient China. Recently, however, China's state food authorities have banned imports of kimchi from South Korea after finding parasite eggs in the imported side dish.

炮轰 (pào hōng)
bombard with criticism

The Chinese term, "bombing," is often used figuratively to describe the act of bombarding someone or some organization with criticism.

陪读 (péi dú)
student guardian/companion

In early times, this term referred to a youngster who was assigned to be a study mate for the offspring of a rich family. Nowadays, it is used to describe anyone who accompanies a child or spouse during his/her study overseas.

捧车族 (pěng chē zú)
car grooms

Some young car owners refrain from using their vehicles whenever a bicycle will do or public transport works just as well. They make the best use of their car rather than abusing them.

捧角 (pěng jué)
star making

It refers to the phenomenon of creating a star by using all kinds of means, especially in the show business.

捧杀 (pěng shā)
excessive praise, liberal extolment

The Chinese term is composed of two words "praise" and "kill." When media shower excessive praise upon a person in the limelight, they unintentionally throw obstacles in the way of his or her advancement in career or simply kill their future.

碰瓷帮 (pèng cí bāng)
porcelain-crashing gang

The Chinese term refers to those who intentionally throw themselves onto or in front of a driving car to get compensation. The term employs the word porcelain because it's fragile and could be costly.

碰钉子 (pèng dīng zi)
hit a snag, get snubbed

It's painful to bump into either end of a nail. The Chinese term, meaning literally "bumping into a nail," is often used to describe the situation in which one's plan either hits the wall or gets snubbed. If you are "politely" rebuffed by others, we say you have bumped into a "soft nail."

辟情操 (pī qíng cāo)
highbrow chat

It's quite trendy these days for young men and women to find a private place in a teahouse, bar or restaurant to chat casually on highbrow topics such as art, philosophy and human emotions. Sometimes, such talk can become quite chummy.

劈腿 (pī tuǐ)
two-timing

This term is frequently used by young people to describe someone who's not faithful to his/her spouse or lover. But a more popular Chinese saying, *jiaota liangtiao chuan*, portrays a two-minded person as riding on two boats simultaneously with each foot on one boat. The latter is often used in a broader sense.

啤酒眼 (pí jiǔ yǎn)
beer goggles

Through a drunken eye, things do look different. Under the influence of alcohol, people tend to choose sex partners they would never prefer while sober. No wonder people say "beauty is in the eye of the beer holder."

漂婚 (piāo hūn)
false marriage

It refers to the kind of extramarital affairs that takes place in a place away from the hometown of both lovers, but it takes on the appearance of a legal marriage.

漂书 (piāo shū)
bookcrossing

The practice of leaving a book in a public place to be picked up and read by others, who then do likewise, has appeared in some districts in the city.

飘一族 (piāo yī zú)
drifting generation

Those who give up their decent jobs to pursue their career dreams are called the drifting generation. They will move to wherever hope of dream come true is beckoning them. They live on odd jobs, mostly freelance, and live in rented houses, varying from a shabby shed way to a serviced apartment.

票友 (piào yǒu)
amateur–pros

In old days, traditional Chinese opera performers were placed on the lower rungs of the social ladder. Some high–class people good at the art only performed as a hobby, rather than a way of eking out a living like professional opera singers. These days, any amateur performers who can beat pros are also referred to as a *piaoyou*.

拼车 (pīn chē)
carpool

While carpooling is encouraged in many big cities around the world to tackle rush hour traffic jams and reduce pollution, some Shanghai city government departments recently drew criticism for banning the practice because it disrupted the taxi service market.

拼一族 (pīn yī zú)
the pooling clan

Urban young people in China are expanding the carpooling to Go–Dutch–type cost sharing of glossy magazines, pricey dinners, promotion coupons and whatever else they feel is too expensive if they pay alone.

平安信 (píng ān xìn)
all-is-well note

Some earthquake survivors tried to send out paper slips from cut-off areas to tell relatives they were still alive and safe.

屏蔽门 (píng bì mén)
metro barrier door

The city plans to install the barrier doors at 12 major stations along the Metro Line 1 by the end of this year to save energy and protect the safety of passengers, particularly during the rush hours.

苹果派 (píng guǒ pài)
Apple fans

The Chinese term translates literally "apple pie," but it's often used to refer to people who are addicted to Apple's products, such as iPhone, iPod and iTunes.

平价时装 (píng jià shí zhuāng)
high-street fashion

It refers to those fashion brands like Zara and H&M that are popular with average-income workers for their trendy design but reasonable prices.

Q

七夕 (qī xī)
Qi Xi Festival

It's the seventh day of the seventh month in the Chinese lunar calendar. Chinese legend says farmer *Niu Lang* (the Cowboy) and his wife *Zhi Nü* (the Weaving Girl), who is actually an angel from heaven, are allowed to meet once a year on the day after their secret marriage is discovered by her heavenly family.

脐带血 (qí dài xuě)
umbilical cord blood

Huang Xinxia, a 28-year-old woman from Anhui Province, is now waiting to see if the umbilical cord blood from her second boy, who was born in Shanghai a week ago would help save her first son, who suffers from leukemia. Doctors at Shanghai No.1 People's Hospital collected the umbilical cord blood, and hope there will be a better chance of a match of stem cells between two brothers.

奇客 (qí kè)
geek

The Chinese term, created according to the sound of the English word, literally means "a strange guest." One doesn't have to be a computer expert or specialist to become a geek. If you are a computer aficionado with a free and unorthodox thinking, people call you a geek.

起步费 (qǐ bù fèi)
base rate, initial meter charge

Shanghai last year raised the taxi base rate from 10 yuan for the first three kilometers to 11 yuan and the additional kilometer rate from 2.0 yuan to 2.1 yuan to offset the soaring prices in the world and domestic oil markets.

起蓬头 (qǐ péng tóu)
sudden pickup

This is a colloquial term used mainly in Shanghai area and the local dialect to describe something, such as sales or activities, beginning to pick up momentum quickly. It also implies a bit of hullabaloo.

气球贷款 (qì qiú dài kuǎn)
balloon loan, balloon payment mortgage

This term refers to a mortgage which does not fully amortize over the term, leaving a big "balloon payment" at maturity. It is a new product introduced by some domestic banks in face of the sluggish mortgage market.

掐尖 (qiā jiān)
take the cream

People these days use the term to refer to the practice of some of the nation's top universities which have the privilege to enroll the best high-school graduates from across the country before others. The Chinese term means literally to nip off the top of a plant's stem or branch.

千手观音 (qīan shǒu guān yīn)
an office with too many chiefs

The Chinese term originally refers to a Buddha called the "Thousand-Handed Avalokitesvara." Since Chinese tend to call leaders "first hand," "second hand," "third hand" and so on according to their ranking in an organization, now this term is also used to mean an office with too many chiefs or too many "hands." For instance, media last week reported that the government of a poor county has one magistrate and 15 deputies.

潜规则 (qiǎn guī zé)
hidden rules

People say hidden rules are the unspoken cues that dictate behaviors and actions. But in colloquial Chinese, the term is often used with a derogatory connotation. For instance, many people believe that only by offering doctors a "red pack" (gift money wrapped in a red envelop) can they expect satisfactory medical services from them.

潜绩 (qiǎn jì)
inconspicuous achievement

Most officials try to make tangible achievements while in office that can help enhance their popularity and gain promotion. But this Chinese term refers to outcomes which are not immediately obvious, but will bring long term benefits.

潜歧视 (qiǎn qí shì)
tacit discrimination

It is a deep-rooted habitual discrimination harbored by one group of people against another though it has never been publicly stated.

潜水 (qiǎn shuǐ)
lurking

This popular expression in the online world refers to the fact that some visitors only read remarks posted by others in the chat room but never participate in the talk.

潜台词 (qiǎn tái cí)
subtext, implication

This term refers to the tacit message of people's remarks or behavior. To get the message, one has to read between the lines or interpret the insinuation.

腔调 (qiāng diào)
aura, manner

The word means an accent or tone of expression in Mandarin but takes on a rich array of meanings in Shanghai dialect. It can refer to polished taste in clothing, well-paced elegance in behavior, sleek manner in spending, or even well-acclaimed style in handling a tricky issue. It can also mean a special kind of attitude.

枪手 (qiāng shǒu)
ghost test-taker, ghost writer

Gunman is the direct translation for this Chinese term, but it is now used metonymically to describe anyone who sits in examinations for others for a fee. The government has been trying very hard to stamp out ghost test-taking, which has become widespread around the country.

强档 (qiáng dàng)
prime time

Prime time is the block of time with the most viewers and is generally when television networks and local stations attract the largest audience and reap much of their advertising revenues.

抢抢族 (qiǎng qiǎng zú)
online bargain hunters

Some young people are hooked online and keep an eagle eye on the limited number of gifts and bargains offered by a business and lose no time to take the offer and get the services.

抢沙发 (qiǎng shā fā)
sofa grabbing

Despite varying etymological accounts, it is generally agreed that the first person to post a follow-up comment or article after the thread starter assumes a sofa, implying a comfortable or important position. It is said it comes from a person who says "so fast" as a response to a responding comment immediately after the threat starter posts an article. The second follow-up comment poster will 坐板凳 (zuò bǎn dèng), or sit on a bench, implying a less comfortable or important place.

抢注 (qiǎng zhù)
preemptive registration

When the name of a celebrity or a famous organization is used for a brand name like "Clinton" condom and "*bushi* (Bush)" diaper, an original advertising effect is secured. A Chinese condom factory's application states television is still awaiting the go-ahead.

敲门砖 (qiāo mén zhuān)
door opener, stepping stone

The colloquial expression literally means a brick used to knock open a door. It is used figuratively to indicate an effective means for gaining access or seizing an opportunity.

桥博客 (qiáo bó kè)
bridge blog

It is the name of online blogs that are playing the role of bridging different cultures. For instance, YeeYan, which provides information from the English world for Chinese speakers, is one of such blogs.

撬边 (qiào biān)
friendly persuasion, false bid

The term originally means to sew the hem of a dress, but it is now often used to imply offering friendly persuasion or staging false bids for someone.

翘课 (qiào kè)
cutting classes

Five foreign students were expelled from the Shanghai University of Finance and Economics for not attending enough classes in the current semester.

跷跷板效应 (qiào qiào bǎn xiào yìng)
seesaw effect

Just like a seesaw back and forth, Chinese mainland investors are usually rushing between the real estate market and the stock markets. Due to the recent boom in China's stock markets, many mainland investors have siphoned household savings out of their property investment.

禽流感 (qín liú gǎn)
avian flu or bird flu

The World Health Organization has warned that the economic impact from a flu pandemic would be enormous and urged countries to prepare for a possible outbreak like the 1918 one that killed 50 million people.

Q

清凉装 (qīng liáng zhuāng)
revealing clothing

It refers to women's summer wear that reveals a lot of skin. However, these days, people have expanded its meaning to any moderately sexy clothing.

情侣装 (qíng lǚ zhuāng)
couples dress

The term refers to lovers or couples wearing matching clothes. It's a kind of fashion-for-two idea.

情绪食品 (qíng xù shí pǐn)
mood food

This is a new trend in the functional food sector. The theory is that diet can affect people's happiness and general wellbeing, affected by the chemical stimulation of neurotransmitters within the brain, resulting in a good mood. Products in this category include "mood-modulating chocolate" produced in the United Kingdom and "pressure-relieving milk" in Japan.

穷游 (qióng yóu)
budget tour, tight–belt tour

The expression refers to the type of traveling that some urban residents undertake out of town on a very tight budget, like eating snack food they buy at supermarkets instead of dining out and staying in a cheap hostel or a farmer's home.

秋乏 (qiū fá)
autumn fatigue

It refers to the phenomenon that many people feel fatigued though not ill at the beginning of the autumn season. Some recent traffic accidents were attributed to this phenomenon.

去中国化 (qù zhōng guó huà)
de–sinicizing

Taiwan authorities headed by Chen Shuibian have taken a series of "de–sinicizing" moves, aiming to create a social climate for the so–called "*de jure* Taiwan independence" scheme.

圈友 (quān yǒu)
Internet social networking, exclusive circle member

Due to lack of time to mix with others in real life, many white-collar workers have become quite interested in social networking in cyberspace. Some create platforms or "circles" for Netizens of common interest, but they tend to be selective on the "circle membership."

全武行 (quán wǔ háng)
acrobatic fighting, scuffle

The term originally means the acrobatic fighting in traditional Chinese operas. These days it refers to the undue fighting or violence at a public place such as in the street or a parliament hall.

缺钙 (quē gài)
stupid

The Chinese term literally means "lack of calcium." Calcium is an important element in one's body, so if you say someone is suffering from lack of calcium, you are actually calling him stupid.

群租 (qún zū)
collective renting

Most migrant workers like to participate in the collective renting program as they cram as many people as possible into a small house in order to cut the share of the rent each has to pay.

R

惹火 (rě huǒ)
inviting, hot

The expression is especially used these days by youngsters to refer to sexy and attractive dresses or ladies with curvaceous bodies.

热裤 (rè kù)
tight pants

The word applies particularly to the tight-fitting short pants worn by young Chinese women who prefer to show off their curves, if any. Usually the pants are worn in hot weather, which may explain why the Chinese word for hot, *re*, is used.

人来疯 (rén lái fēng)
get hyped before crowd

Many children tend to close their usual self and turn unruly when guests drop by. It is also used to describe the rarely exhibited showy behavior of an adult at the presence of a crowd of strangers.

人脸识别系统 (rén liǎn shí bié xì tǒng)
facial recognition system

Beijing announced lately that it will equip a facial recognition system in 500 shopping malls to improve security measures during the 2008 Olympic Games.

人脉 (rén mài)
connections

Ren literally means a human and *mai*, veins and arteries, which are traditionally deemed essential to good health. Some experts say friendships and other personal relations may push an entrepreneur a solid step toward success.

人气 (rén qì)
popularity

When a place attracts a large crowd on a regular basis or is always full of activities, people say it is enjoying high popularity, or in Chinese, it is full of "human smell."

R

人球 (rén qiú)
helpless castaway

The term, literally meaning "human ball," refers to poor people for whom no one is willing to provide help. They are kicked around by people just like a tattered football. The term "little human ball" describes those kids whose parents have divorced and neither is willing to look after them.

人性化服务 (rén xìng huà fú wù)
people-oriented service

The city's service industry has been promoting a "people first" practice in order to provide more considerate and satisfactory services to clients.

肉机 (ròu jī)
hacker-controlled computer

This term, "meat machine" as it translates literally, refers to a hacker-controlled computer which has been infected with some sort of malware.

软创新 (ruǎn chuàng xīn)
soft innovation

This term refers to innovation of macro or micro management systems. They include operation mechanisms, management, policies, organization, business model and production process.

软骨症 (ruǎn gǔ zhèng)
"soft bone" syndrome

This refers to the phenomenon of some authorities conniving at malpractice by their subordinates after taking bribes from them.

软脚蟹 (ruǎn jiǎo xiè)
spineless, namby-pamby

Soft-legged crab, as this term literally translates, is no good because it's premature and yields little meat. It is often used to describe a person deemed a weakling.

软肋 (ruǎn lèi)
soft spot, Achilles' heel

The word literally translates as a soft rib, but Chinese people use it to represent the most vulnerable spot of a person, a program or system.

软实力 (ruǎn shí lì)
soft power

From *Soft Power: The Means to Success in World Politics*— a book written by Joseph Nye, who was said to create the concept in the 1990s. Soft power is the ability to get what a country wants by attracting and persuading others to approve and support its goals.

软文广告 (ruǎn wén guǎng gào)
advertorial

The Chinese term translates literally as "soft–article advertising." It derives from the English word "advertorial," a portmanteau of "advertising" and "editorial." Advertorial is an advertisement presented in the form of a legitimate and independent news story in a publication.

软性技能 (ruǎn xìng jì néng)
soft skill

In addition to professional know-how, an employee will be viewed favorably by an employer if he or she possesses personal qualities such as good communication and expression skills and a strong team spirit.

软装 (ruǎn zhuāng)
soft decoration

The arrangement of potted plants, framed photos, oil paintings and other artworks or accessories in a house is called soft decoration, as compared to the interior decoration featuring plumbing and flooring.

润物女 (rùn wù nǚ)
woman of active life

This is a phrase coined by Chinese and used as the opposite to the Japanese term "himono onna" or "dried-fish woman." The Japanese term refers to a female who has little activity other than staying home and spending time online. They pursue a simple lifestyle and shy away from complicated social networking. The Chinese term refers to women who love going out, keep fit and enjoy life.

S

3F危机 (sān F wēi jī)
3F crisis

This new term refers to the financial crisis, fuel crisis and food crisis now plaguing many parts of the world.

三股势力 (sān gǔ shì lì)
"Three Forces"

Shanghai Cooperation Organization member countries signed 10 documents, including an agreement on cutting off the infiltration channels of the "Three Forces," namely terrorists, separatists and extremists at a summit meeting on June 15, 2006 in Shanghai.

三夹板 (sān jiá bǎn)
sandwich husband

Due to the Chinese cultural background, the mother-in-law and daughter-in-law are usually deemed as sworn enemies. If a man is caught in the war between his mother and his wife, he is often likened to a "three-ply board," as this Chinese term means literally, because the middle layer of a three-ply is tightly squeezed between the two outside layers.

三明治一族 (sān míng zhì yī zú)
sandwich clan

It refers to those urbanites aged between 35-45 who are "sandwiched" between their parents and children. They have to work hard to earn enough money to guarantee a decent life for their families.

三手烟 (sān shǒu yān)
third-hand smoke

It refers to smoke stuck in the walls, tables or other objects. You feel it when you come close to those objects. Third-hand smoke is no less harmful than first-hand or second-hand smoke. Third-hand smoke has been found to be a major cause of lung cancer.

散养 (sǎn yǎng)
course-free vacation, relaxing vacation

This Chinese phrase originally means "free range" or raising animals in a free roaming manner. Now the term is used to describe a vacation for a child who is not forced to take any extracurricular courses or art lessons either by their teachers or parents.

散伙饭 (sàn huǒ fàn)
goodbye dinner

This is a popular way among college students to say goodbye to each other when they graduate. They always drink a lot in the dinner and laugh or cry to show their reluctance to part. Many restaurants near campuses all across China are banking on such dinner parties during this season.

扫货 (sǎo huò)
shopping spree

With the upcoming Christmas and New Year's Day, most stores in Shanghai have already begun the annual sales season by offering big discounts. As a result, some customers plan to start their shopping spree in the manner of "sweeping away the goods," as the term means.

扫街 (sǎo jiē)
street sweeping

Street sweeping does not just mean to clean the street any more. Now it can be used to describe activities involving a complete scrutiny of shops or people in a street. Tourists could sweep a street by visiting every food stall or bar there and paparazzi could sweep a street by closely watching everything moving there to wait for an exclusive shot.

色友 (sè yǒu)
shutterbug

Enthusiastic amateur photographers in China call themselves *seyou* or "colorful friends." They claim they are a bunch of people who love anything that's colorful. Don't try to translate this Chinese term without a real understanding of it, because the first character in the term can also mean "lascivious."

沙尘暴 (shā chén bào)
sandstorm

Sandstorms that swept Beijing and other northern cities have worsened the air quality of 50 percent of China's already most polluted cities.

杀青 (shā qīng)
clinch, wrap

The term literally means degreening, a process to treat fresh tea leaves. The term is also used to depict a method of baking bamboo slips more than 2,000 years ago in preparation for them to be written on. Today, however, it is often used to describe wrapping up a film shoot or in a broader sense, clinching a project.

杀手锏 (shā shǒu jiǎn)
trump weapon

In ancient China, *jian* was not a very common weapon, but if someone could use it skillfully, it would prove to be a surprisingly decisive one. Today, the Chinese term *shashoujian* means a trump weapon, which is rarely used before.

杀熟 (shā shú)
friend hacker

This term refers to those who make use of their friends' trust to rip them off. They usually sell to their friends or relatives products including cosmetics, tonics and even insurances at a price higher than the market tag.

煞根 (shà gēn)
shocking, extreme

The Shanghai dialect is one of the typical examples of the Chinglish developed in the colonial period of Shanghai as *shagen* is a near transliteration of the English word shocking. It may also roughly translate as extreme.

晒工资 (shài gōng zī)
disclose one's salary

The Chinese term vividly compares disclosure of a person's salary to airing the salary sheet under the broad sunlight. Many people now like to disclose their salaries in detail—often anonymously—on the Internet, to complain how little they earn.

晒黑族 (shài hēi zú)
injustice exposer

It refers to Netizens who team up to expose social injustice or corrupt officials by posting articles on the Internet in the hope of attracting attention from authorities, and urging them to take action.

晒客族 (shài kè zú)
self-disclosing clan

The expression refers to the cluster of Netizens who are ready to expose anything private, from salary details to personal property to their children's academic achievements, on the Internet.

晒密族 (shài mì zú)
secret displayer

This term refers to people who reveal their secrets on Websites. The secrets can be salaries, their hatred of some person, and unhappiness at work.

山寨版 (shān zhài bǎn)
cheap copy

This term, meaning literally the "mountain village edition," is widely used to describe cheap copies of any known products, programs, events or even architecture. It was first applied to cheap imitations of brand name cell phones produced by individuals or small shops in southern China and now it refers to an inexpensive copy of anything that's well known or popular.

闪 (shǎn)
pop off, leave

The Chinese character means to "flash" or "duck." It is now often used by Netizens in online chatting to mean "leaving" or "avoid doing something."

闪婚 (shǎn hūn)
flash marriage

In a metropolis like Shanghai, speed is everything. So, the "eight-minute speed daling" has become quite popular, particularly among young white-collar workers. Over the weekend, several hundred single men and women participated in a "flash marriage" event, hoping to find their Mr/Miss Right there and then tie the knot in a matter of days or even hours, if not minutes.

闪客 (shǎn kè)
flash mob, flash artist

These people are "gathered" through the Internet. They perform a specific task in an assigned place at an assigned time. After that they just disappear. The Chinese term also refers to those animation artists using flash software.

闪离 (shǎn lí)
flash divorce

As more and more people flirt with speed dating and speed marriage, the inevitable spinoff is a quick divorce.

闪约 (shǎn yuē)
flash appointment

It refers to a blitz kind of meetings between single men and women. Arranged by a go-between agency, a man would talk to a girl he never met before for only 20 minutes, and then he mush dash to the next appointment and talk to another girl for no more than 20 minutes. He can meet several girls in such a flash way to find his best love. Wow. You try.

善客 (shàn kè)
charity blogger

This term refers to people who sign onto a charity Website to donate money to the needy or set up blogs for charity purposes by using their real names.

上海利率 (shàng hǎi lì lǜ)
Shibor/Shanghai interbank offered rate

China starts a new interbank offered rate between banks, which acts as a domestic benchmark for borrowing and is modeled after the London interbank offered rate, or Libor. Shibor is set by 16 lenders making bids for borrowing and cover maturities from overnight to one year.

上镜 (shàng jìng)
photogenic

If you always look your best on a picture, it is a case Chinese people call "*shangjing*," which literally translates as "on lens."

上网本 (shàng wǎng běn)
netbook

Netbook refers to a spate of newly popular laptop models that are light-weight, low-cost, power-efficient and highly portable. Netbooks are suitable for Web browsing, email and general purpose applications. They typically have weaker processing power, smaller screens and hard-disks than full-featured notebooks and have limited ability to run resource-intensive operating systems.

少女系男生 (shào nǚ xì nán shēng)
sissy boys

It refers to those young males who resemble their female peers both in look and behavior.

蛇夫座 (shé fū zuò)
Ophiuchus

Some people support the introduction of Ophiuchus (November 30–December 17) as the 13th sign of the zodiac in order to correct calendar calculation errors. Meaning "snake–holder" in Greek, Ophiuchus would be inserted between Scorpio and Sagittarius.

涉黑 (shè hēi)
gang–related crimes

Chinese rock musician Zang Tianshuo has been arrested by Beijing police for a suspected role in several gangland activities. It is the tip of a social problem in which a few government officials and celebrities are in cahoots with local gangsters.

社会化书签 (shè huì huà shū qiān)
social bookmark

This term refers to an online bookmarking system where users store lists of useful Internet resources. Such lists are accessible to the public or a specific network.

身价 (shēn jià)
showbiz value, personal wealth

An online poster recently published a detailed list of the market value of popstars in China, including Hong Kong, Macao and Taiwan. The Chinese term also refers to the wealth of a business person.

审美疲劳 (shěn měi pí láo)
aesthetically blasé

Because of frequent exposure to or indulgence in something beautiful, one may gradually become less excited or even uninterested. Chinese director Feng Xiaogang's hit movie *Cell Phone* has helped the expression gain popularity on the Chinese mainland.

肾结石宝宝 (shěn jié shí bǎo bǎo)
kidney stone baby

It was recently brought to light that thousands of infants in China developed kidney stone diseases after taking melamine-tainted milk formula. Melamine, which may lead to reproductive damage, or bladder or kidney stones if ingested, has been found in a few milk powder products prepared for infants.

生白族 (shēng bái zú)
life idiot

This term refers to youth who cannot handle their daily chores, such as washing clothes, folding quilts, cooking food, and even tying shoe laces, because of their parents' over indulgence. Such young people are "idiots in life," the literal meaning of the Chinese term.

生活家 (shēng huó jiā)
life–ist

The pompous term is popular with those who claim to know how to make the best of their life, even on a meager income.

生活作风问题 (shēng huó zuò fēng wèn tí)
unethical lifestyle, loose morals

In corruption cases, more often than not the perpetrators are charged with having a "lifestyle problem," a euphemism for loose morals, especially in their sex lives. An unethical lifestyle is one of the reasons cited in a Communist Party document for the sacking of Shanghai Party Secretary Chen Liangyu in 2006.

生猛 (shēng měng)
undaunter, unfearing

The word is often used to describe young people who are a bit overoptimistic about the future and know no fear. They are usually smart and energetic, but a bit "raw" and immature.

生肖票 (shēng xiāo piào)
zodiac stamp

At the beginning of each of year, the Chinese post office faithfully publishes sets of stamps to mark the zodiac animal of the new year on the Lunar Calendar. More than 100 enthusiastic philatelists lined up overnight last week at Shanghai Postal Museum to buy newly-issued stamps to commemorate the Year of the Dog.

剩女 (shèng nǚ)
left on the shelf

It refers to those highly-educated and well-paid successful career women who, for whatever reasons, have not found their Mr Right at an age traditionally believed way past the best getting-married years. The Chinese term translates literally "leftover girls."

尸体货 (shī tǐ huò)
corpse goods

Some online buyers complain that the products, most second hand, they purchase from others are thoroughly broken, functionless or cannot be used any more. Such goods are called corpse goods, which have already "died" and have no "second life."

失写症 (shī xiě zhèng)
computer-induced agraphia

This is a newly emerging "illness" among people who use computers all the time. Its symptom is the partial loss of the ability to write correct Chinese characters with pen and paper. Unlike usual agraphia, a disorder marked by loss of the ability to write, it has nothing to do with brain damage and can often be cured if the "patient" is willing to pick up the pen and paper again.

实话实说 (shí huà shí shuō)
talking straight, plain speaking

This Chinese phrase has become very popular partly due to a well-like namesake TV program on China Central Television. Nowadays, people often quote this phrase when they prepare to shoot straight.

什锦八宝饭 (shí jǐn bā bǎo fàn)
Jin–Bao fans

The fan club named after a Chinese dessert is actually a fan base of Chinese President Hu Jintao and Premier Wen Jiabao. The official website of the *People's Daily*, run by the Chinese Communist Party, created a special site for them, called "Jin and Bao Fans" (http://politics. people.com.cn/GB/8198/132796/index.html) on September 4 in 2008.

实体店 (shí tǐ diàn)
real shop

Nowadays, some people tend to run "real" shops on street corners alongside with "virtual" shops on their Websites. The purpose is to win trust and business from more customers.

食物里程 (shí wù lǐ chéng)
food miles

This term means the "mileage of food" before it reaches the consumer. According to a study report, the rise in food miles has led to increases in the environmental, social and economic burdens associated with transport, which include carbon dioxide emissions, air pollution, congestion, accidents and noise.

屎坑贼 (shǐ kēng zéi)
toilet thief

Police in Foshan, Guangdong Province, recently detected 20 robbery cases that all happened in public toilets. This term is a moniker of criminals who rob or steal valuables from people using toilets.

试客 (shì kè)
free product tester

Many Websites now start to offer free products, such as shampoo and make-up, as test samples to anyone who registers. However, testers have to write feedback reports about the quality of the product or their ideas about it. This information, in turn, will be sold to producers.

试民 (shì mín)
product tester

This term refers to people who agree to test new products or services provided by manufacturers or companies. They are either paid for doing the test or allowed to keep the products provided to them. But they are usually required to submit feedback on the quality or usage suitability of such products and services.

收官 (shōu guān)
draw to a close

People have borrowed the term from the Chinese game "go" to refer to an event that is coming to an end or conclusion.

收声 (shōu shēng)
shut up

The Chinese expression, once often used in formal context, is now frequently used at online platforms and media publications to mean stop talking or discussing.

收支两条线 (shōu zhī liǎng tiáo xiàn)
separate channels of revenue and expenditure

Following a recent pension fund scandal, Shanghai

has issued a new regulation to separate the management of the money in revenue account from that of the money in expenditure account to avoid future misuse of the city's pension fund.

手办 (shǒu bàn)
in-action figure

The term "in-action figure" refers to plastic figurines modeled on comic book or science fiction characters. These figurines are normally 10–30 centimeters in height and produced in small quantities.

手滑了 / 手抖了 (shǒu huá le/shǒu dǒu le)
slip of fingers

The Chinese phrase means "a slip of hand" or "a shivering hand." This phrase is often used to explain a simple typo in writing as, more often than not, office workers are using keyboard to type text into computers.

首席忽悠官 (shǒu xí hū yōu guān)
CHO

The H here is short both for "human resources" and the

Chinese pinyin for *huyou* (or coaxing). Young people playfully call the human resources workers as CHO these days because they believe in many cases the HRs are trying to paint a rosy picture of their companies for job seekers, against the fears of a global economic recession.

瘦身 (shòu shēn)
slimming, streamlining

The term of getting slimmer has been generalized to mean reducing the size of almost anything. It could be streamlining government departments, shrinking investment plans or even reducing the weight of school kids' satchels.

枢纽站点 (shū niǔ zhàn diǎn)
public transport transfer depot

Shanghai plans to build 60 new public transport transfer depots by 2010 to streamline transfers between metro lines, buses, private cars, railways and even flights to promote the city central transport position in the Yangtze River Delta region.

淑女学堂 (shū nǚ xué táng)
finishing school

This refers to some newly established schools specializing in teaching girls and women traditional ladylike manners, including playing lute, Chinese painting and writing poems.

淑商 (shū shāng)
gentlewoman quotient

Modern men prefer a woman to have more merits than just being gentle and having good manners. The ideal women should also be well-educated, funny, psychologically and economically independent, among others. However, the question is how many men deserve a lady of such a high gentlewoman quotient.

书托 (shū tuō)
book shill

Chinese Website Douban.com, a reputed social network service Website featuring online book reviews, is troubled by the intervention of professional shills. These people are hired either to boast about a certain book or attack books published by rivals.

熟年 (shú nián)
mature-aged

This term refers to people who are between 45 to 64 years old. In urban areas, this group of people boasts consumption power and consciously follows new trends. However, they also face problems in job, retirement, health, marriage and sex life.

熟女 (shú nǚ)
sophisticated lady

The term refers to a woman between 30 and 50 who has proper manner, a decent job, rich experience in life and well-polished taste in fashion.

熟女文学 (shú nǚ wén xué)
chick lit

It is the abbreviation of "chick literature." Chick lit is a type of novels that are written by young women and for young women readers. Heroines in these stories are spike-heeled, single and professional women, who search for their positions in big cities, just like those in *Sex and the City*.

树洞贴 (shù dòng tiē)
tree hole post

It is said that in the past, people tended to dig a small hole in a tree, hide their secret in it and then seal it with mud so no one else would know it. Today, in the virtual world of cyberspace, many love to post their secrets on the Internet anonymously. It makes them feel just like hiding their secrets in tree holes. Some may also find it stimulating to see others' response to their secrets.

数独 (shù dú)
sudoku or number place

This is probably the most popular logic puzzle around the world today. The aim of the puzzle is to fill in each empty square of a grid of 81 cells so that the figures 1 to 9 appear just once in every row, column and individual 3*3 block. Though sudoku is a Japanese name, the puzzle's true modern origin lies with a team of puzzle constructors in 1970's New York. Check out the sudoku column on C6 in *Shanghai Daily*.

数码痴呆症 (shù mǎ chī dāi zhèng)
digital amnesia

This term refers to people who rely too much on digital

products, such as mobile phones and computers, so their memories deteriorate.

数字家庭 (shū zì jiā tíng)
digital home

The term means a fully automated residence. China is trying to help more and more families have access to Internet services and other home appliances powered by digital technology.

刷票 (shuā piào)
ballot rigging

The term means stuffing the ballot box with countless fraudulent votes. As public ballot is becoming a popular mechanism in electing popstars in TV entertainment programs in China, vote frauds are also on the rise. Some have even created special ballot-rigging software.

刷屏 (shuā píng)
screen flooding

The term refers to a case where a Netizen floods the screen in a chat room, a forum or BBS by repeatedly posting the same text or pictures in order to block others from posting their messages. It's a kind of "online filibuster."

耍大牌 (shuǎ dà pái)
throw around a celebrity's hauteur

Some celebrities believe that they are entitled to demand the impossible, to abuse reporters, to act rudely to fans and to treat most people around them as inferiors.

衰退达人 (shuāi tuì dá rén)
recessionista

The term refers to those who are adept at changing their consumption habits during the severe economic downturn. Contrary to the "fashionista" who are in blind pursuit of labels, they advocate a kind of thrift–permanent, steady, moderate and positive consumption in order to minimize the impact of a recession. They are expert in sourcing discounts to buy what is cheap but chic.

甩手掌柜 (shuǎi shǒu zhǎng guì)
hands-off manager

The phrase refers to owners or managers who don't actively participate in their business, instead letting others take care of the daily chores for them. The term may also be used to describe "do-nothing" government departments or a person who does not lift a hand at home.

双规 (shuāng guī)
double-designation

This term means a special investigation scheme of the Communist Party of China when a member or official of the Party is ordered to make explanation or confession about his/her alleged involvement in a discipline-violation or corruption case at a designated time and in a designated place.

双核家庭 (shuāng hé jiā tíng)
dual-core family

This refers to a family where both husband and wife are only children or the single "core" of their respective families before they got married. The new family, of course, has two "cores" as neither of the couple knows how to behave not as a "core" in a family.

双开 (shuāng kāi)
double dismissal

This term is often used to describe an official who is expelled from the Communist Party of China and removed from his/her office at the same time for serious violation of disciplines. Double dismissal is meted out as a severe punishment for those wrong-doing officials if they are Party members.

双面胶 (shuāng miàn jiāo)
peacemaking husband

Contrary to the "three-ply board" (三夹板 sān jiá bǎn) as described in the previous entry, "twin adhesive," as this Chinese term translates verbatim, refers to a man who smoothens the relationship between his mother and wife and keeps a harmonious family just like the "twin adhesive" used to glue two different objects into one.

水货 (shuǐ huò)
grey import

It is also know as a parallel import, which is made available in the local "grey market" by retailers who order the trademark goods directly from overseas wholesales at a lower price and without going through official import channels. Most such imports are shipped to the local market by water, hence the Chinese term, *shuihuo* (water goods).

睡会族 (shuì huì zú)
habitual dozer at meetings

This term refers to people who always snooze during meetings, partly because the meeting is long and boring.

睡眠博客 (shuì mián bó kè)
dormant blog

The term refers to those blogs that are rarely updated by their writers. Statistics show that on average, over 70 percent of blogs are not updated each month.

睡眠机器 (shuì mián jī qì)
sleep machine

The high-tech machine is designed to treat insomnia by physically stimulating some part of insomniacs' brains to help them quickly enter a state of deep sleep.

私房菜 (sī fáng cài)
private home cuisine

Sifangcai or "private home cuisine" has become a fad in many large cities around the country. It's a kind of home catering that features traditional family recipes in a setting just like home.

私房钱 (sī fáng qián)
pin money, egg money

This term refers to a small amount of money one earns and has stashed away for future spending for oneself behind the back of his/her spouse.

私了 (sī liǎo)
out-of-court settlement

Parties sometimes tend to settle disputes among themselves without going to the court or authorities to save trouble or to avoid bad publicity. Drivers in Shanghai are now required to settle disputes over minor accidents by themselves instead of calling for police to help in order to speed up traffic flow.

私享家 (sī xiǎng jiā)
person of free spirit

The word is a homonym with "thinker" in Chinese and means literally a "person of private enjoyment." But it actually refers to people who pursue health, leisure and an independent lifestyle. They have their own ideas, pick their own place to stay and share leisure time with family and friends, but always keep some time for their own. They also tend to maintain a place of privacy in their heart and try to "privatize" their enjoyment.

死党 (sǐ dǎng)
sworn friend

The Chinese expression originally means a diehard follower but is often used these days by youngsters in reference to their own very close friends who they believe will never let them down in whatever situation.

死机 (sǐ jī)
stunned, dumbfounded

Netizens borrow the Chinese term for an unexpected computer shutdown to refer to the state when people are too stupefied by an occurrence to respond.

搜救犬 (sōu jiù quǎn)
rescue dog

Rescue dogs are reportedly more reliable and stable than a life detector for their sharp olfactory sense in finding disaster survivors.

素婚 (sù hūn)
frugal wedding

Instead of traditional lavish wedding extravaganza, some young couples nowadays choose to take plain ways to mark their marriage. They usually participate in a simple group wedding ceremony or just take a honeymoon trip somewhere, skipping all the big banquets and exhausting, costly ceremonies.

素历 (sù lì)
personal quality resume

Instead of a sum-up of one's education, this term means a summary of a person's quality training, particularly in terms of organizational and leadership capability, positive work attitude, communication skills, stable mental health and willingness to learn and progress.

素人 (sù rén)
layman, bungler

The term refers to those who know little about a field, a job or hobby, or those who are only just dabblers that are prone to blunders.

素质场 (sù zhì chǎng)
Cheat-you-out-of-your-pocket place

The term literally means "a place of quality." It refers to some restaurants or other entertainment venues where sexy women lure men into unreasonably expensive services, such as a small glass of ordinary wine for an astronomical price. These women, however, never go to bed with men. Cheated men often cannot complain, as they are lured by sex in the first place. These men are then ironically called "men of quality."

素质教育 (sù zhì jiào yù)
all-round education

Many Chinese educators, parents and politicians have long been calling for a fundamental reform in the country's education system in order to eradicate its numerous flaws rooted in traditional exam-oriented schooling. They say what the country needs is an all-round education system to help bring forth millions of young people with a well-balanced moral, intellectual and physical education, not just examination machines.

T

她经济 (tā jīng jì)
she economy

Women have become the biggest players in many consumer markets and business sectors in comparison with men. As a result, some economists believe they are upholding more than half the sky in the economy of a growing number of countries.

踏青 (tà qīng)
spring outing

The Chinese term vividly depicts one who merrily goes on a trip in spring. *Ta* means "step on" or "walk by," while "*qing*" means the greenness of grass. For hundreds of years, *taqing* has been associated with the tomb sweeping activities around the *Qingming* (Clear and Bright) Festival, which falls on April 5.

太超过世代 (tài chāo guò shì dài)
exceptional generation

The term, first publicly used by Peggy Chiao, chair-woman of Taiwan's Golden Horse Film Awards and well-known movie critic, refers to a group of young Taiwan directors. The word "exceptional" here means extremely talented and outstanding. This generation of directors includes Wei Te-sheng, who made *Cape No.7*, a blockbuster Taiwanese hit.

太空人 (tài kōng rén)
frequent jet traveler

Some people like businessmen or popular showbiz artists who have to, or like to, fly around the world frequently.

太太团 (tài tài tuán)
WAG

The term refers to the wives and girlfriends (WAG) of sportsmen that fly to a match to encourage their husbands and boyfriends, a common sight in the Western sports scene.

T

碳补偿 (tàn bǔ cháng)
carbon offset

After introducing the concept of the carbon footprint, here's a term meaning how to compensate for some amount of carbon dioxide that someone or something has added to the atmosphere. It could be making a donation or simply planting more trees.

碳足迹 (tàn zú jì)
carbon footprint

Carbon footprint is a measure of the amount of carbon dioxide emitted through the consumption of fossil fuels. It is the impact that businesses, organizations or individuals make on the planet from the use of energy.

唐僧肉 (táng sēng ròu)
everyone's craving

The Chinese word derives from the classic novel *Journey to the West*, which describes how Monk Tang (Tripitaka) went to the West to find the Buddhist scriptures. It is said that anyone who eats Monk Tang's flesh will become immortal. As a result, every devil in the novel tries to capture the monk and eat his flesh. Today, the term refers to any lucrative business or opportunity where everyone wants to have a taste of the dish.

糖水片 (táng shuǐ piàn)
aesthetic photo

The term translates literally as a "sugar water photo." It refers to the portrait or scenery photos that feature aesthetic techniques and superficial beauty but lack significance or meaning. "Sugar water" sounds similar to "Pond water" in Chinese and the latter is deemed by some shutterbugs as a sine qua non in scenery photos.

饕客 (tāo kè)
gourmet

The Chinese term is a bit humorous. It is not just about any gourmet. It refers to a gourmet who eats in wild joy.

掏空族 (tāo kōng zú)
hollow clan

The term refers to people who are so overworked that they have no time for recharging themselves through continuing-education or training. They tend to become "hollow" because they are burning out all their knowledge, energy and enthusiasm they had accumulated in the past.

淘浆糊 (táo jiàng hú)
muddle through

This Shanghai slang dates back many decades and has an origin involving tailors and brothels. But today it is frequently used to indicate anyone who tries to muddle through an unfavorable situation by either muddling someone up or blurring the line between right and wrong.

淘客 (táo kè)
online shopper

The term refers to those who search online for goods they like to purchase via a relatively safe third-party transaction platform. The phrase took off when taobao. com, a local C2C online shopping Website, became more and more popular.

桃色腐败 (táo sè fǔ bài)
sex–related corruption

It refers to the type of corruption of some government officials who take advantage of their positions or illicit income from their power to keep a mistress, womanize or visit prostitutes.

讨债人 (tǎo zhài rén)
debt collector

Six Shanghainese recently obtained debt–collection certificates after taking courses at a professional training center. The center is authorized by the Ministry of Labor and Social Security to train debt collectors in six fields, including state regulations and negotiation skills.

特困生 (tè kùn shēng)
super–sleepy student

The Chinese expression literally means a student from an extremely poor family. But it is now often used on campuses to refer to students who often take naps during the class. The middle character in this Chinese term means "poor" here, but it sounds the same as another Chinese word meaning "sleepy."

特型演员 (tè xíng yǎn yuán)
lookalike actor

China's film authorities have a tradition of setting up a pool of actors who resemble late Chinese leaders like Mao Zedong and Zhou Enlai. One such actor, Wang Lixian, a Mao Zedong lookalike from Liaoning Province, died recently in a road accident in Taiwan during the National Day holiday.

体商 (tǐ shāng)
body quotient

It has come to refer to the health state of a person these days as more people pay increasing attention to their physical well-being.

天价 (tiān jià)
whopping price

The Chinese term literally means the price is as high as the sky. An old man who is treated in a local hospital in Harbin, Heilongjiang Province last summer had to pay an unbelievably high price of 5.5 million yuan (US$680,000). Many expenses were later found to be fabricated by the hospital.

天葬 (tiān zàng)
celestial burial

Celestial burial is a funeral that has been practiced for more than 1,000 years in Tibet. Celestial practitioners feed a dead body to vultures, which they call holy eagles. The Tibetan government has recently decided to better protect the custom by banning photographing or making videos of celestial burial scenes.

贴吧 (tiē bā)
online post bar

It's a rising method among fans to set up an online bar to publish posts related to their idols. By typing the name of an idol, you can easily find the person's bar on Baidu and if not, you can be the first one to establish the bar.

贴牌 (tiē pái)
original equipment manufacturer (OEM)

This term means a manufacturer that makes products for its clients with its clients' brands. Many Chinese companies grow by working as OEMs for overseas companies. In the latest example, Japanese electronic maker Sanyo Electric Co has agreed to let Haier Group, the Chinese mainland's biggest home appliance maker, become its only original equipment manufacturer of refrigerators.

贴秋膘 (tiē qiū biāo)
flesh out in autumn

Traditionally, autumn is a harvest season and thought of as a season of plenty. Also, the cool temperature brings back the appetite of many people who lost weight in the long, sweltering and often sleep-depriving summer. Therefore, autumn is also a good season for people to recover and store up much needed energy.

贴身媒体 (tiē shēn méi tí)
personal media

It refers to mobile phones that carry news in the form of broadcasting short messages (SMS) or multimedia messaging service (MMS).

铁头功 (tiě tóu gōng)
head butt

France captain Zinedine Zidane was redcarded in the 110th minute of the World Cup final for head butting Italy defender Marco Materazzi in the chest. Zidane claimed that he was provoked because Materazzi insulted his mother and sister.

通吃 (tōng chī)
fix-all

The word is believed to have come from gambling when someone has a landslide winning hand or a game where winner takes all. These days, people also use it to refer to a silver-bullet solution or tactic.

通心粉 (tōng xīn fěn)
macaroni people

The name of pasta in any of various hollow shapes is now used to describe people who are impressive in appearance but disappointing in substance. It's similar to the English saying "Many a fine dish has nothing on it" or the Chinese idiom "embroidered pillow," which boasts a beautiful cover, but with only worthless dried straw stuffed inside.

偷着乐 (tōu zhe lè)
laugh in sleeve, covert pleasure
It is the case when you are happy about something but you don't want to share it with others or when you are sure of a future happy thing that nobody else is aware of.

偷着胖 (tōu zhe pàng)
unnoticeably fat, a hidden fatty
Those who don't look fat with clothes on, but are actually quite plump are called a hidden fatty in northern China. It takes great efforts to be secret about one's subcutaneous fat these days when revealing clothing is in, especially for young women.

头像 (tóu xiàng)
avatar
This term refers to the model or icon used in the chatrooms, MSN, QQ and other online communities or games, to represent a user or participant. It's usually a three-dimensional model in computer games or a two-dimensional icon in Internet forums.

土食者 (tǔ shí zhě)
localvore

Localvore refers to people who eat only locally grown food. The idea is to save on the fossil fuel that is used to transport out-of-season foods for thousands of kilometers. The localvore movement has been in vogue for the past couple of years in the West.

土食族 (tǔ shí zú)
locavore

A locavore is someone who eats food grown or produced locally. The locavore movement encourages consumers to buy from farmers' markets or even to produce their own food, with the argument that fresh, local products are more nutritious and taste better.

兔爸 (tù bà)
tool bar

The term literally means "rabbit papa," because it have a similar Chinese pronunciation with "tool bar" — a bar of useful buttons usually at the top or on the left side of the interface of a software.

吐槽 (tù cáo)
debunk, gibe

The expression means to debunk or show up the false nature or ridiculousness of someone's remarks, especially in front of others. The phrase is believed to originate from the Japanese term "tsukkom."

团购 (tuán gòu)
group purchase

Some people like to form a group to buy things, like furniture, cosmetics, automobiles, digital cameras and even houses at a wholesale price. Shanghai Volkswagen Co has issued China's first co-branded credit card in the automobile industry to offer discounts for auto buyers. Card holders can enjoy value-added services, including test driving, group purchase, favorable auto financing and car maintenance.

团子 (tuán zi)
panda

The Chinese term is one of the nicknames for panda and it literally means dumplings. People use this to describe the round-shaped, fatty pandas. Other popular nicknames include Gungun (滚滚), which means rolling in Chinese, also used to describe roly-poly pandas.

推手 (tuī shǒu)
promoter

It refers to a person who helps bring another to stardom before anyone else discovers the potential value of the latter. An organizer of an event or crusader can also be called a promoter.

推优生 (tuī yōu shēng)
recommended students

It refers to straight-A students who are recommended for enrollment into a senior high school or a university without taking entrance exams like their peers.

退耕还林 (tuì gēng huán lín)
grain for green project

In order to restore the ecological balance in west China, the central government has initiated a program to offer grain subsidies to local farmers and encourage them to turn low-yielding farmland back to forest and pastures. The Chinese government has allocated 61.7 billion yuan (US$7.63 billion) for this project over the next five years.

托大 (tuō dà)
preen oneself, self-boasting

The Chinese term literally means "entrusting oneself too much." This colloquial term is often used in an informal and humorous way.

脱女博客 (tuō nǚ bó kè)
blog stripper

The phrase refers to those female bloggers who go to the desperate length of posting their scantily clad or even nude pictures online to attract visitors and gain fame.

陀飞轮手表 (tuó fēi lún shǒu biǎo)
tourbillon watch

Tourbillon, invented by French watchmaker Abraham Louis Breguet in 1795, is a technology which improves a watch's accuracy by nullifying the effect of gravity using a series of mechanisms. Shanghai Watch, a history-honored brand, recently introduced its first 50 limited edition tourbillion watches. They were purchased almost instantly.

娃妈 (wá mā)
doll mommy

This term refers to some young women who spend a lot of time with ball-joint dolls. They "adopt" (buy) dolls and treat them like their own kids. The dolls, mostly made in Japan and South Korea, look realistic and cuddly with large heads and big eyes.

娃娃音 (wá wá yīn)
doll voice

This term refers to a special sweet, cute and doll-like singing style. A typical example is model-turned-actress Lin Chi-ling, who however says she has learned to grow out of the voice after starring in *Red Cliff*.

外挂 (wài guà)
cheating program

Cheating programs are designed to help players skip

some tough or tedious steps in an online game to accumulate more experience points. Such programs make the games easier to play, but they may deprive players of the excitement in online games.

玩心跳 (wán xīn tiào)
play heartbeat

The two Chinese words in this term are "play" and "heartbeat." When you decide to play with your heartbeat, you're about to engage in exciting and often dangerous activities that that will quicken your heartbeat and cause an adrenalin surge. Bungee jumping is a good example of such activities.

玩转 (wán zhuàn)
having command of, being adept in

The two Chinese characters in this term are "play" and "spin." So, if one has learned to "play" a game and can make it "spin," he is deemed as having a good command of the skill. Actually, the term can be used for any skill, practice, profession or operation.

晚尚 (wǎn shàng)
evening fashion

This newly coined term with the same pronunciation as the Chinese term for "evening" actually means fashion activities in the evening.

晚托班 (wǎn tuō bān)
after-school care service

Many working parents share a common plight in being unable to find suitable carers for their young children after school until they get home in the late afternoon. Now, some organizations such as the neighborhood committees have established after-school care centers for the youngsters.

万金油 (wàn jīn yóu)
jack of all trades

Originally, this was the name of a palm ointment used in traditional medicine to treat many minor problems. But it can never cure any real illness. Therefore, people use it to refer to someone regarded as a jack of all trades.

网格员 (wǎng gé yuán)
grid inspector

This actually refers to city inspectors introduced in Shanghai's Luwan District. Armed with a specially designed handy GPS mobile phone, the inspectors cover their respective designated area by walking a grid. They will report any "abnormalities," such as traffic jams, misplaced garbage bags, a missing manhole cover and other eyesores, to the control center. The center then will decide how to deal with the reported problems.

网恋 (wǎng liàn)
BBS love, virtual love

Internet-based love is also one of the spin-offs of the modern world. It either comes to nothing, grows into true love, or plays into a cunning hand.

网络草根 (wǎng luò cǎo gēn)
netroots

This term is a portmanteau of Internet and grassroots and refers to political activism organized through blogs and other online media. Many attribute US President-elect Barack Obama's election victory partly to his "netroots" campaign.

网络电话 (wǎng luò diàn huà)
VoIP

VoIP, or Voice over Internet Protocol, is a method to turn analog audio signals into digital data that can be transmitted over the Internet. By using some of the free VoIP software, one can make Internet phone calls by bypassing the phone companies as well as their charges.

网络钓鱼 (wǎng luò diào yú)
phishing

This term refers to the activity of using social engineering techniques to fraudulently acquire sensitive information, such as passwords and credit card details, in an electronic communication. Phishing is usually carried out by using e-mail, fake Websites, copy-cat Web pages or an instant message.

网络黑帮 (wǎng luò hēi bāng)
cyber gang

Recently, some cyber hackers have blackmailed Website owners by attacking their Websites with DDoS, or Distributed Denial of Service, and demanded money or consultancy "fee."

网络视频女郎 (wǎng luò shì pín nǚ láng)
camgirl

This term refers to a girl or young woman who broadcasts live pictures of herself over the World Wide Web. Nowadays, more people are choosing to live in front of a camera, hooked up to the Internet via a high-speed connection. Most of them are girls and young women broadcasting from the most private spaces of their bedrooms, bathrooms and living rooms.

网络推手 (wǎng luò tuī shǒu)
Internet star-maker

This Chinese term refers to people who use the Internet to create new stars in various fields by bringing someone into the spotlight of public attention from oblivion.

网申 (wǎng shēn)
apply online

Internet has saved job applicants the trouble of whirl-wind visits to human resources offices of companies but the flip side of the story is that only a precious few of their applications on the Internet will get an answer.

微博客 (wēi bó kè)
Twitter

A service to communicate through the exchange of quick, frequent answers. Users send short messages to mobile phones and groups of Websites instead of one individual.

威客 (wēi kè)
witkey

The term refers to Websites which provide online Encyclopedia services, such as Google answer, Wikipidia, Sinai ask. In China, witkey Websites are still new. With only a year of development, the number of users has reached about 600,000, with a monthly surge of 30 percent.

维实 (wéi shí)
wikiality

This term is a translation of a new English word "wikiality," which means a reality as defined by a consensus, particularly in a collaborative online endeavor such as Wikipedia. Any user can change any entry and if enough other users agree with them, it becomes true.

围堰 (wéi yàn)
cofferdam

China last week demolished the last cofferdam which protected the main wall of the Three Georges Dam on the Yangtze River in central China's Hubei Province. The removal of the top of the temporary structure means the Three Georges Project has formally begun its role in flood control, two years ahead of schedule.

尾货 (wěi huò)
surplus goods

This term usually refers to textile goods made of leftover materials from contracted production of brand-name products, products originally manufactured for export, or knockoff products made by manufacturers of customer-ordered products. They are usually sold to retailers at lower-than-cost prices.

伪球迷 (wěi qiú mí)
biased fans, follow-suit fans

Soccer or basketball fans who spare no effort to promote their favorite teams or players but speak ill of all others are called biased fans. The term may also mean people who just follow the behavior of true fans to share some excitement.

伪文化 (wěi wén huà)
pseudo culture

It often refers to the creation of artificial tourist attractions or the promotion of business events in the name of culture.

尾牙 (wěi yá)
year-end dinner party

Evolved from a tradition in southern Fujian Province for worshiping the god or a standard of colors, many employers have turned the last worship ritual in a year into a dinner party to treat their employees. It is particularly popular in Taiwan.

伪中产 (wěi zhōng chǎn)
pseudo-middle class

This term refers to those asset-rich and cash-poor salary earners who have a few "middle class" symbols, such as a suburban house and a private car, but don't have much cash at their disposal. It may also refer to those "all work and no play" people who are too busy making money to enjoy a middle-class life.

味道美女 (wèi dào měi nǚ)
belle waitress

The Chinese term literally means "delectable beauty." And many gourmets believe that beautiful waitresses are the sine qua non of a fine feast.

温吞水 (wēn tūn shuǐ)
tepid, apathetic

This phrase has been used as a colloquial expression in Shanghai dialect for many decades and remains very alive in everyday conversation today. It refers to a person who lacks interest or enthusiasm in doing things or tends to go about duties or chores at a snail's pace.

文化奶妈 (wén huà nǎi mā)
cultural nanny

The term originally referred to Yu Dan, a female professor who explained difficult traditional Chinese literature and moral classics to the public in plain language on a TV program. Now the term refers to anyone who feeds the public with highbrow culture like a nanny feeds a baby.

窝案 (wō àn)
collective corruption

This term refers to a corrupt act carried out via the collusion of a group of people, who usually work in the same work unit or department.

窝边草 (wō biān cǎo)
nest–side grass

A rabbit would not eat grass around its nest, as an old Chinese saying goes. The traditional adage advises people never to harm their neighbors if they want to go a long way.

沃客 (wò kè)
work 2.0

This is a new type of Internet–based service trading market. Companies or individuals may post their assignments (usually for graphic design, logos or innovative ideas) on a Website and anyone may bid for the assignments. Some people call work 2.0 the "business version" of Web 2.0.

乌鸦嘴 (wū yā zuǐ)
jinxing mouth

Chinese believe the crow cawing could bring an unlucky spell on people. So, anyone who has a jinxing mouth is said to have a *wuyazui* or "crow's mouth," a persona non grata in any conservation or discussion.

无厘头 (wú lí tóu)
meaningless act

The phrase derives from "*moulaitou*" in Cantonese, which was first used to describe a trend in Hong Kong pop culture started by actor Stephen Chow. His brand of slapstick comedy features exaggerated body language, trash talk and black humor. Now any absurd, meaningless and anomalous approach to express one's opinions or feelings can be described as "*wulitou.*"

无烟工业 (wú yān gōng yè)
smokeless industry

Smokeless industries, such as tourism, design and fashion industries, are considered environment-friendly industries which are particularly suitable for megacities like Shanghai. Also, they can bring in big money without causing harmful pollution.

物权法 (wù quán fǎ)
property law

Since China has modified its constitution and launched protection of personal property rights, the country began to draft its first property law to implement the protection of people's legal properties. The law has been passed by the National People's Congress.

嘻哈包袱铺 (xī hā bāo fú pù)
hip hop crosstalk society

This refers to a group of mostly amateurish crosstalk performers who have won acclaim among young audiences in Beijing recently. Almost all the performers are in their 20s and they lard their comedy talk with hot buzzwords and pungent online terms.

吸金 (xī jīn)
money spinning, money making

This term translates literally "sucking gold." It actually refers to any enterprise, project or person that rakes in a lot of money.

洗澡蟹 (xǐ zǎo xiè)
bathed crab

Late autumn and early winter is the season for hairy crabs, one of the most favored delicacies of people living in Shanghai and its surrounding areas. Among hairy crabs, those produced from the Yangcheng Lake are deemed as the very best and people are willing to pay big money for them. Crooked dealers, however, tend to bring in cheaper, and perhaps inferior, crabs from other places and dip them in the Yangcheng Lake for a few days or weeks. They then sell those "bathed crabs" as the genuine product for higher prices.

戏霸 (xì bà)
despot actor/actress

It is a term to describe some big-name actors or actresses who throw their weight around and look down their noses at film directors and other performers and often demand unreasonable treatment.

虾米 (xiā mǐ)
what

On a BBS, this popular word means "what." It came from China's southern Fujian dialect, which pronounces "what" in Chinese similar to "*xiami*" — dried small shrimps.

下沉式广场 (xià chén shì guǎng chǎng)
sunken square

A sunken square that serves as a pedestrian access to shops around the busy crossing of five major roads in Yangpu District recently opened. Entertainment facilities are also available at the square.

下流社会 (xià liú shè huì)
iPod generation

The Chinese term originally means the demiworld or low-life society. But now, it is used in Japan to refer to young people who are living under financial and social pressure and having little enthusiasm for life or progress in any field. Meanwhile, a new term "iPod generation" has appeared in UK, referring to young people who live an "insecure, pressured, over-taxed and debt-ridden" life.

下猛药 (xià měng yào)
drastic measures

When people adopt drastic measures to solve a nagging problem or a widespread social headache, the act is preferred to as a case of *xiamengyao*. The expression literally means to "prescribe a strong medicine" for a serious ailment.

下三赖 (xià sān lài)
riffraff, low–class

Many Chinese students tend to use the literal English translation of this term, "down three bad." As a translation, it's not bad, since it conveys almost the right sense. In daily conversation, however, the term is widely used to express scorn.

咸潮 (xián cháo)
salt tide

The tide takes place at the mouth of the Yangtze River every winter or early spring, when water flowing from the river decreases, causing chloride level to rise and even exceed the national standard. Local media reported the year's first salt tide in the East China Sea may threaten one of Shanghai's two sources of fresh water during the Spring Festival.

咸猪手 (xián zhū shǒu)
salty pig feet, groper

Taiwan and Guangdong people refer to a man who tends to pay unwanted sexual attention to a fair lady as "*zhuge*," which translates literally as "pig brother." Hence, the hands (or "feet") of the man who takes advantage of overcrowding to grope female passengers (or female colleagues in offices) are called *xianzhushou*.

现代病 (xiàn dài bìng)
money spinning, money making
This term translates literally "sucking gold." It actually refers to any enterprise, project or person that rakes in a lot of money.

现金池 (xiàn jīn chí)
cash pool
This is a sophisticated system for managing funds for corporations. It optimize the interest results of a group of businesses. China Merchants Bank in October initiated the foreign exchange cash pool, the first of its kind on the Chinese mainland.

现实空间 (xiàn shí kōng jiān)
meatspace
This Chinese term derives from the English word meatspace, a tongue-in-cheek term used as an ant-

onym for the term cyberspace. It refers to real life or the physical world.

香蕉人 (xiāng jiāo rén)
banana

This term refers to the overseas Chinese who are born abroad and grow up in foreign and particularly Western countries. They have Asian looks, but are totally Westernized in thinking and life style.

消费名片 (xiāo fèi míng piàn)
well-known tourist program (or venue)

Many Chinese cities have made big efforts to promote their best programs and venues to tourists and visitors. They call them the "name card for consumption."

消费税 (xiāo fèi shuì)
excise tax

The nation hopes the revised excise tax which started on April 1, 2006 to levy on cars, as well as other luxury products, will control the number of sedans on the roads as part of its effort to cut energy use and rein in air pollution.

小报告 (xiǎo bào gào)
sneak on, snitch

Most people think of "filing little secret reports," as the Chinese term literally means, as despicable behavior. But in reality, quite a few people, adults or kids alike, would resort to this ploy to win trust or favor from their superiors and trash their peers.

小大人 (xiǎo dà rén)
an old head on young shoulders, mature beyond one's years

The Chinese term, a little adult, is usually used to describe a child who behaves as if he is much older and more mature than his age. It's a commendatory term used to praise a child for being exceptionally smart or understanding.

小混混 (xiǎo hùn hùn)
dawdling punk

This Chinese term is derogative. It refers to teenagers

or young people who do nothing but hang around.

小人书 (xiǎo rén shū)
picture storybook

Books contain pictures matched with word, which are popular among children because they are easy to understand. Many classic editions have become very expensive now.

小字辈 (xiǎo zì bèi)
obscure person

Compared with big shots or people of a higher status, fledgling artists or people at the grassroots level of a company are often called *xiaozibei* .

校草 (xiào cǎo)
school beau

This term translates literally as "school grass," the male counterpart of the "school flower (campus belle)." So, naturally, it refers to the most handsome and attractive male student on the campus.

笑场 (xiào chǎng)
laugh-out-loud, LOL

A widespread online phrase, whose abbreviation is LOL, mainly refers to a movie scene that was designed to win people's sympathy but instead generates a laugh.

校漂族 (xiào piāo zú)
campus drifters

Those who have finished college but still are addicted to the simple life in the ivory tower are called campus drifters as they stay on the campus whenever possible to avoid social life or pursue academic progress.

歇菜 (xiē cài)
come on, hit a wall

The slang expression commonly used in Beijing and other northern regions is a mild way of telling someone to stop doing or saying something others find disagreeable. It may also be used to say someone's hitting a wall.

协保人员 (xié bǎo rén yuán)
social security–guaranteed laid–off workers

This term refers to workers who have agreed to be laid off, where their former employers have in return agreed to pay their social security contributions for an agreed period.

谐音成语 (xié yīn chéng yǔ)
homophonic idiom

A growing number of advertisers like to play with Chinese idioms by replacing them with different but homophonic Chinese characters to suit their commercial purposes. Some linguists warn that such practice could "contaminate" the language, particularly, among young students.

写真集 (xiě zhēn jí)
photo album

It literally means a collection of portraits, but in daily talk it often refers to the photo albums of popstars or other celebrities. The trend is they are showing more and more flesh in such albums.

心灵超市 (xīn líng chāo shì)
soul–soothing supermarket

This term refers to stores selling empty bottles, bags and containers bearing words such as "No more pressure!" "Sleep eight hours" or "Wanna happy weekend." The buyers use these containers to carry water or other daily necessities as a way to alleviate their mental stress.

心水 (xīn shuǐ)
favorite

This term originally meant "idea," "thinking" or "mood" in Buddhist scriptures and ancient poems. Now, Cantonese as well as many people in other parts of the country use it to describe anything or anybody that wins your heart.

新新人类 (xīn xīn rén lèi)
new–new generation

This is a term for a "novel generation" of youngsters who have novel ideals, are always ready to try out new fashions and new lifestyle, do whatever they see appropriate and are willing to be responsible for their unconventional action.

信息洁癖 (xìn xī jié pì)
ungoogleable

This term refers to a person for whom no information appears in an Internet search engine, particularly Google. This is because either the person purposely makes himself or herself anonymous on the Internet or he/she doesn't exist. The term can also refer to the fact that a word, name, place or thing cannot be found through online search engines.

型男 (xíng nán)
metrosexual men

It refers to the modern metropolis men who spend a considerable amount of time and money grooming their appearance to look decent and sexy.

性福 (xìng fú)
sexual satisfaction

The term has the same pronunciation as that of "happiness" in Chinese. But the newly-coined term here actually means sexual satisfaction, not any other form of "happiness."

性情中人 (xìng qíng zhōng rén)
unsophisticated person

The Chinese term means someone who speaks one's mind and acts in a natural and honest way. He or she does not calculate before he or she speaks up or takes actions.

休车日 (xiū chē rì)
alternate no–car day

Chinese cities like Shanghai and Beijing have enacted rules to curtail use of some official and private cars on certain days according to their license plate numbers in an effort to alleviate traffic congestion and pollution.

秀豆 (xiù dòu)
short

The Chinese term is based on the Japanese pronunciation of the English word "short." Originally, it means short circuit, but now it describes someone whose brain suddenly stops functioning and can't even work out simple problems.

虚火 (xū huǒ)
inflated price, superficial glory

"Hyperactivity of the fire," or "false fire" as translated literally, is the term for an illness in traditional Chinese medicine with a symptom of a dry tongue. But the Chinese word "fire" in this sense can also mean "glory" or "popularity" or "high price." If you believe some products are sold at inflated prices, you may say those products are having "false fire."

虚拟经济 (xū nǐ jīng jì)
fictitious economy

This term refers to transactions involving securities, futures and financial derivatives. Due to the current global financial crisis, this term appears frequently in newspapers and daily conservation. It is the opposite of the "real economy" or "substantial economy."

虚拟奴隶 (xū nǐ nú lì)
online slave

"Buy me as your slave" is now a greeting among some Chinese online users. Similar to "Friends for Sale" application in www.facebook.com, this application offered by www.kaixin001.com gives users a whole new experience compared with other run-of-the-mill social networking Websites. www.kaixin001.com is a new entrant to the Chinese SNS (social networking service). At "Friends for Sale" each user can be sold as a "slave" twice every day through the virtual payment system. The "Owners" can earn money by forcing the "Slaves" to work as singers, miners or toilet cleaners. Or, they could just be "tortured" for fun.

穴居动物 (xué jū dòng wù)
cyberspace troglodyte

The term, which means cave animals in Chinese, is a new phrase evolved from the development of the Internet and online communication. Many young people are inclined to stay at home all the time. They talk to others, order food or do everything they want through the Internet.

学院风 (xué yuàn fēng)
preppy style

This term means a dress style that can be traced back to students or graduates of expensive preparatory schools in the United States. It includes denim shirts, V-necked sweaters and pencil trousers.

雪藏 (xuě cáng)
stash, freeze

This Chinese term means literally to bury something in snow. It often refers to the tactic of benching a team's top players in order to conceal its strength and save them for future, bigger battles. But it may also describe the situation when singers and movie stars are pulled out of the spotlight by their employers.

血汗工厂 (xuè hàn gōng chǎng)
sweatshop

The Chinese term, a "blood–sweat factory," is used to describe a workplace where employees are forced to work long hours under poor conditions and with very low pay.

血拼 (xuè pīn)
shopping

This Chinese term literally means a "bloody fight," but sounds similar to the English word that it stands for. In a commercial metropolis like Shanghai, shopping is a craze and can be "bloody." Many of the city's shopping malls, supermarkets, stores and restaurants open 24 hours a day over the New Year holiday and saw all their floors constantly packed with shoppers.

血头 (xuè tóu)
blood–sale ringleader

The "blood head," as this term translates literally, refers to ringleaders who organize illegal blood sales in some poor areas in the country.

循环课本 (xún huán kè běn)
used textbook

The Chinese term, "recycled textbook," actually means used books as you see in many US colleges. Some Shanghai schools have begun to promote used books to save resources.

Y

丫客 (yā kè)
grassroots artist

It refers to people or "grassroots artists" who have a special interest in art, especially music. They usually have their own Web pages or blogs on yeskee.com to show off their talent and communicate with their peers.

压岁钱 (yā suì qián)
red packet, lucky money

In ancient China, people tended to put some copper coins wrapped in red paper beside the pillows of their children on the Lunar New Year's Eve to drive away a devil called "*sui*." It has evolved into today's red packet or lucky money that parents and older relatives give to children during the Lunar New Year to wish them good luck.

压洲 (yā zhōu)
pressure continent

This phrase's pronunciation is similar to "Asia" in Chinese, but it means a continent of pressure. It is now used as a nickname for modern Asia as it has undergone great pressures from the faster pace of life, deeper shortage of raw materials and higher risk of pollution.

鸭子 (yā zi)
light traveler

The word "duck" is used here for those tourists who travel light and tend to join a tour group organized by travel agencies. They are like ducks herded around by the guide.

鸭子舰队 (yā zi jiàn duì)
drifting rubber ducks

This term refers to hundreds of thousands of Chinese-made rubber ducks which dropped into the water after a sea accident in 1992. After 15 years of floating on the sea, many of these rubber bath toys have been washed up on the shores of North America and

Europe. One division is expected to invade Britain's shores next year. Their prices have skyrocketed.

哑巴亏 (yǎ bā kuī)
take it on the chin

The Chinese term, "a dumb man's loss," refers to someone who suffers losses or grievances but is forced to keep it quiet, or stay "speechless," because of existing circumstances.

亚腐败 (yà fǔ bài)
sub-corruption, gray-area corruption

It refers to the kind of corruption, especially some hidden forms of bribery, that is not specified in criminal law but is still punishable. Typical examples are government officials taking expensive artworks as gifts or using and actually possessing cars "lent" to them by their "personal friends."

亚健康 (yà jiàn kāng)
semi-health

Semi-health conditions are half way between good

health and ill health. Such conditions, including headache, insomnia, stiff shoulders and chronic constipation, are often diagnosed as symptoms of illness, but they are deemed by TCM doctors as warning signs of health deterioration or harbingers of ill health.

亚熟男 (yà shú nán)
semi-mature man
Men who look mature but are actually a few steps away from being psychologically grown-up.

颜文字 (yán wén zì)
smiley character, emoticon
In online communication, more and more Chinese tend to use characters resembling facial or emotional expressions. Many have already been created in writing and in the so-called "textspeak."

眼吧 (yǎn bā)
eye-health bar
This is a kind of optometry clinic where a computer-

manipulated environment claimed to be beneficial for eye health is created to help ease eye stress and disorders.

堰塞湖 (yàn sè hú)
quake lake

A lake formed when a river is blocked by rocks from landslides following an earthquake.

洋漂族 (yáng piāo zú)
foreign drifter

As China keeps opening its doors wider to the outside world, more foreigners come to invest, work, study or travel in China. But some wander from one city to another for different jobs and to experience different cultures, and they are called "foreign drifters."

养牛族 (yǎng niú zú)
jeans lover

In Chinese, jeans can be translated literally as "cattle boy's pants." So, jeans collectors are now called *yangniuzu* or "cattle breeders." To get a unique color and style, they seldom wash their jeans and try to wear their pants as long as possible. In their words, they use their body to "raise" a special pair of jeans.

养眼 (yǎng yǎn)
eye–candy

This term is an expression used to describe something or someone that is very pleasant to the eyes, including a movie or computer game with incredible graphics and visual effects or a young woman with a very pretty face and attractive figure.

摇新族 (yáo xīn zú)
IPO chaser

Profit–minded stock investors who chase only lucrative initial public offering while shunning listed shares offerings. This is a special condition in China because share prices always rise on the debut trading day.

YAWN族 (yawn zú)
YAWN clan

The initials stand for young and wealthy but normal, a label given to sensible young people who refrain from overspending or driving a car for environmental reasons.

野鹅族 (yě é zú)
wild goose clan

To ensure their children learn "real" English, many parents in South Korea bring their children to English-speaking countries to study. Usually, the mother lives with and takes care of the child during the overseas study trip, while the father stays behind earning money to support the family. They get together only during vacations.

夜店 (yè diàn)
nightclub

The Chinese term derived from Taiwanese parlance. The term literally means "night shop."

一把手 (yī bǎ shǒu)
chief leader, first chair

The Chinese term means the first in a pecking order. Due to the stunning pension fund scandal that hit the city last year, the Shanghai municipal government has urged closer supervision of all chief leaders in government departments, institutions and state-run enterprises.

一刀切 (yī dāo qiē)
across-the-board ruling

It refers to a rule or decision made by a government or a company that allows no exception when being enforced in order to achieve good effectiveness or to avoid unfairness.

一哥 / 一姐 (yī gē / yī jiě)
top gun

Top gun is the most famous and influential person in a sector, especially in the entertainment industry, such as movies, music or variety shows. The Chinese means the first brother or the first sister.

一肩挑 (yī jiān tiāo)
multi-tasker

The term in Chinese is often used to describe a person who, just like a multi-function device, plays at least two different roles in his or her daily work and life. For example, an able mother can work both as a housekeeper and an office lady, so that her children can live happily. It also refers to some Chinese officials, who act as both the administrative head and the Party chief of a unit.

医闹 (yī nào)
medical dispute profiteer

Some people nose around for medical disputes and encourage the patient to file a lawsuit against the hospital. They hire more people to pretend to be the relatives of the patient during the legal procedure and claim part of the damage awarded.

一枪头 (yī qiāng tóu)
one-shot kill, do it in one go

It is a Shanghai dialect that means you succeed at one try, just like a one-shot kill.

一条龙服务 (yī tiáo lóng fú wù)
all-in-one service package, turnkey service

The expression refers to the services a business offers a client or customer, featuring "start-to-finish" arrangements.

医托 (yī tuō)
hospital scalper, hospital stoolie

The city police crack down on scalpers selling registration numbers at major hospitals as well as touts who lure people from major hospitals to small, lesser-known and even unlicensed facilities.

一招鲜 (yī zhāo xiān)
trump card

This Chinese term refers to any unique skills, products or ways of doing thing that can bring you success wherever you go.

以房养房 (yǐ fáng yǎng fáng)
rent-for-mortgage scheme

Some people lease out their spare apartment and use

the revenue to defray their monthly mortgage for another property.

以房养老 (yǐ fáng yǎng lǎo)
house-for-pension scheme

This term refers to a new scheme to increase the income of senior citizens in the city. People who are 65 or older are qualified to sell their home to the city's Housing Fund, but they can continue to live in it by paying a market-level rent to the fund. Although different from the reverse mortgage scheme, it also allows seniors to access the equity in their home.

乙醚 (yǐ mí)
Yi's fan

The Chinese term literally means "ether," but here it refers to the fans of a Chinese literature professor Yi Zhongtian, whose modern interpretation of a classical novel, *The Three Kingdoms*, is quite popular among many readers. The Chinese term sounds like "Yi's fan."

易服 (yì fú)
cross-dress

This term is used to describe people who dress like a member of the opposite sex. Actually, transvestism is not new to the Chinese. Back in the Northern Wei dynasty (AD 386–AD 534) a young woman named Hua Mulan disguised herself as a man to join the army to spare her elderly father of military service.

毅行 (yì xíng)
stamina walk

The Chinese term "*yixing*" refers to a popular outdoor sport in Shanghai, in which people walk a long distance non-stop to exercise and make friends at the same time. The Chinese term derives from the saying of Confucius that a noble man has to cultivate a strong mind.

阴阳公告 (yīn yáng gōng gào)
yin-yang bulletins

In Chinese, yin and yang are used to describe the negative and positive energy in nature. The term may also mean opposing qualities of a phenomenon. So, yin-yang bulletins refer to contradictory statements made by persons or organizations.

阴影 (yīn yǐng)
shadow

It is used these days when someone says he or she is still reeling from the negative influence from a certain event that made him unhappy or unsuccessful.

银保 (yín bǎo)
Bancassurance

Bancassurance is the term used to describe the sale of insurance products in a bank. The word is a combination of "banque or bank" and "assurance" signifying that both banking and insurance is provided by the same corporate entity. In China, more and more banks begin to sell policies on behalf of insurers, and in return give banks certain fees for the service.

银发产业 (yín fà chǎn yè)
silver industry

With a quickly ageing population in big cities like Shanghai, the business that focuses on products and services for seniors is becoming a booming economic sector.

引爆点 (yǐn bào diǎn)
tipping point

In sociology, the tipping point is the moment when something rare in society becomes commonplace. The term was introduced into daily life by Malcolm Gladwell's 2000 bestselling book *The Tipping Point: How Little Things Can Make a Big Difference*. It now also refers to a certain point in any process beyond which the momentum picks up dramatically.

隐婚族 (yǐn hūn zú)
fake singles

Under the pressure of work, some people, especially women between 25 and 35, choose to hide from fellow workers or deny the fact that they are already married as they fear that their married status may bring inconvenience at work and hamper their promotion.

饮酒代驾 (yǐn jiǔ dài jià)
drivers for drunks

During the weeklong holiday, some companies have begun to offer the "You Drink, We Drive" service to help revelers avoid driving while drunk. However, China still lacks relevant rules to regulate such services.

饮水机 (yǐn shuǐ jī)
water dispenser

Local authorities are conducting inspections of water dispensers used in offices and other public places in response to media reports that many such machines have serious quality problems that could create health risks.

印客 (yìn kè)
inker

It is a form of business which can make anyone an "author." People can gather their personal articles and consign the "inker" company to turn them into a book, with pictures they select and pages they design. Such books are not for sale, but to keep as a memento.

婴儿舱 (yīng ér cáng)
baby hatch

It is a kind of incubator–like hatch into which mothers drop the babies they can't take care of. The facility, in use in Germany, Italy and mostly recently in Japan, is designed to protect abandoned babies.

迎峰度夏 (yíng fēng dù xià)
gear up for summer power consumption peak

Shanghai launched a campaign to fight against power shortage in summer, because the city's demands for power reach 20.5 million kilowatts this summer, growing 10.2 percent from a year earlier.

影子艺人 (yǐng zi yì rén)
showbiz doppelganger

This refers to an ordinary person whose facial features resemble a famous artist, allowing him to earn an income from masquerading as the star at low-end parties and gatherings to entertain the audience or guests.

硬骨头 (yìng gǔ tóu)
tough job, tough guy

This term "hard bone" refers to a tough job that is hard to complete. It can also be used to describe people who are tough, hard to beat and unwilling to surrender.

硬伤 (yìng shāng)
inherent problem, glaring mistake

It means an unsolved inherent drawback that undermines an organization, a system, a relationship or a person's integrity. It also refers to those glaring blunders that should be avoided in an artwork, such as misquoted words in a film.

硬柿子 (yìng shì zi)
tough guy

Most people like to eat "soft persimmons" and few fancy "hard persimmons," as this Chinese phrase means literally. But according to a recent popular drama called *I Want to Become a Hard Persimmon,* the soft persimmon is the name of any pushover and the hard persimmon refers to a tough guy.

幽客 (yōu kè)
UFO fans

This term refers to people who believe in the existence of UFO and are addicted to studying this phenomenon.

悠客 (yōu kè)
no-hurry tourist

Those who take their time and don't mind how long they linger at each tourist site or destination.

油价联动机制 (yóu jià lián dòng jī zhì)
fuel-related fare adjustment

At a public hearing held on the effects of rising gasoline prices on the city's taxi fleet, it became clear some adjustment was needed to take the burden off cabbies suffering from an earnings squeeze. Taxi fares have been changed according to the oil prices in the market.

油老虎 (yóu lǎo hǔ)
gas guzzler

"Oil tiger," as this term translates literally, refers to cars that get very poor gas mileage. Many Chinese nouveau riche favor "oil tigers" to show off their wealth.

油条 (yóu tiáo)
flirtatious boy

The phrase, which means fried bread stick in Chinese, is popular among young people, especially those born after 1990, to refer to men who are always flirting with different women.

游学生 (yóu xué shēng)
audit student

The term refers to those students who want to update skills and stay current in their field without seeking academic credit for courses. It may also refer to unregistered students who want to take courses for free. Some of the latter are from poor families who cannot afford the tuition; others are high school graduates who have failed college entrance examinations.

有价无市 (yǒu jià wú shì)
having a price but no sales

This Chinese term actually describes a situation where a product has a fictitious or prohibitively high price but no sales. For instance, many apartments and houses in the city's property market today are so expensive that few could afford or intend to buy them. The term is a little bit satirical.

语言暴力 (yǔ yán bào lì)
verbal violence

Among all types of violence, verbal violence is the most common. Now the term is used to mean slogans, remarks and language used in online discussions that are full of violent and abusive words or expletives.

郁闷 (yù mèn)
angry and frustrated

This term is a favorite among young people these days and they frequently use it whenever they feel "pissed off."

玉米虫 (yù mǐ chóng)
cybersquatter

The term, which means "corn worm" in Chinese, refers to cybersquatters who register, traffick in or use a domain name that's the same as or similar to a famous trademark, company or individuals' names.

They then offer to sell the domain names at an inflated price.

御宅族 (yù zhái zú)
otaku

Otaku is a Japanese term used to refer to a variety of geek, fan boy or fan girl, particularly one obsessed with such hobbies as manga. When applied to a person, it can have either positive or negative connotations depending on the situation and the person using the term.

原生态艺术家 (yuán shēng tài yì shù jiā)
indigenous artiste

This term refers to those rural artists or rather farmers whose performances are rooted in their daily life, without any artificial polish or professional background. Through generations, they have retained the most indigenous elements.

月光族 (yuè guāng zú)
moonlite

This concocted Chinese term is the moniker for people who always spend all their salaries or earnings before the end of the month. The first Chinese character in the term means "month" or "moon," and the second "leaving nothing behind" or "light."

月抛型 (yuè pāo xíng)
monthly dumper

This refers to people who change their dating partners frequently. It borrows its meaning from contact lenses that are tossed after one month's use.

月嫂 (yuè sǎo)
maternity matron

Chinese women traditionally are confined indoors for a month after delivering a baby on the grounds that they are particularly susceptible to various gynecological diseases in this period. During the maternity month, maids, usually married women already having their own kids, are hired to take care of the newborn and the mother.

晕 (yūn)
faint

Originally, the Chinese word means faint or dizzy. But now people tend to utter the word whenever they hear or see something unordinary, confusing, funny or just meaningless.

晕菜 (yūn cài)
stupefied

The colloquial word is used when someone feels at a total loss in an unexpected situation which is beyond his or her comprehension.

云计算 (yún jì suàn)
cloud computing

It is a distributed computing technology, an improvement on Distributed Computing, Parallel Computing and Grid Computing as well as commercial realization of scientific computing concepts. Many famous IT companies such as IBM, Yahoo and Google promote services and products through this technology.

运动电玩 (yùn dòng diàn wán)
exergaming

This term refers to an activity that blends video games with workouts. Some researchers have found that exergaming more than doubled players' energy expenditure compared with sedentary gaming, and suggested that it "might be considered for obesity prevention and treatment."

孕味摄影 (yùn wèi shè yǐng)
pregnancy photography

This term refers to stylish photos of pregnant women. It's a play on the words in Chinese as the first two characters of this term sound similar to a common Chinese phrase meaning "lasting appeal," but the first character now means "pregnancy."

Z

砸星运动 (zá xīng yùn dòng)
star-bashing campaign

After the father of an Andy Lau's fan committed suicide in Hong Kong in early 2007, some young people on the Chinese mainland smashed CDs and tore down posters of pop stars in an attempt to reason with infatuated fans.

赞 (zàn)
superduper

This Chinese word, meaning "to praise," is now widely used on the Internet by Chinese Netizens to extol and recommend a movie, a story or any other things. It conveys the mixed feeling of appraisal, approval, recommendation and admiration.

脏话衫 (zāng huà shān)
clothing with expletives

Clothes printed with English, Japanese and Korean

expletives are popular among local children, especially middle – school students. They think "It's not nice to say these words, but it's cool to wear them." However, their fashion interest at present has worried parents, some of whom even use dictionaries to vet their children's wardrobes.

藏漂族 (zàng piāo zú)
Tibet drifter

Unlike Beijing drifters and Shanghai drifters who start careers in the two cities, Tibet drifters tour the autonomous region then find they can't tear themselves away.

扎台型 (zhā tái xíng)
be showy, act dashingly

When some people feel too good about themselves and go to the lengths to show it off in front of others, they are "acting dashing." This is a Pidgin English term in Shanghai dialect which borrows the English words "dashing."

诈弹 (zhà dàn)
false bomb

This Chinese term has the same pronunciation as the Chinese term for "bomb", but with a twist: the first character *zha* here means "false," not "explosive."

摘客 (zhāi kè)
patchwork bloggers

While some bloggers write their own articles and postings on the Internet, others are regularly copying or compiling others' blogs.

宅内消费 (zhái nèi xiāo fèi)
at-home consumption

With a financial downturn sweeping across the world, it has become a new trend to switch from consumption away from home to consumption at home. It includes eating at home and watching movies at home.

斩冲头 (zhǎn chòng tóu)
rip off a sucker

This is a Shanghai slang, meaning to treat someone as a pushover or foolish spender in a deal or transaction. If you were persuaded to buy something of poor quality at a high price, you would be called *chongtou* (sucker) by Shanghainese.

斩熟 (zhǎn shú)
rip off a friend

It's a not-so-rare phenomenon these days for someone swindling his or her friends, colleagues or even relatives for financial gain. They usually sell fake or substandard products to their friends by abusing the latter's trust and friendship. It's particularly common for those involved in pyramid sales schemes.

蟑螂族 (zhāng láng zú)
cockroach clan

The term is used to describe people who are unperturbed by any negative publicity about them and who insist on living in an environment that is unsuitable for them. Like cockroaches, they have the ability to survive in hostile conditions.

长草 (zhǎng cǎo)
a growing craving

This word is to describe the growing of some consumers' desires for certain items. For example, when a girl is interested in cosmetics, clothes or shoes but can't buy them immediately because of high price or other reasons, her desire will grow until buying them. The Chinese literally means "grass-growing" (in the heart), which reflects the robust growing of the desire for the product.

账客族 (zhàng kè zú)
online-account keeper

Recently, young people tend to operate an online-account book, usually choosing a personal asset-management software or logging onto a specific Web journal. They keep accounts everyday to avoid spending all their salaries or earnings before the next pay day.

账外账 (zhàng wài zhàng)
concealed account

It refers to a secret account a company or work unit keeps outside its official account. This practice is frequently uncovered among some state-owned enterprises, whose managers are bent on chiseling away at state–assets.

朝九晚无 (zhāo jiǔ wǎn wú)
working overtime

This term is created by employees who always work overtime. They have borrowed it from the common phrase of "nine-to-five" working hours and then changed the last character "five" to "no end," since both characters sound nearly the same in Chinese.

招牌菜 (zhāo pái cài)
signature dishes/house special

Dianping.com, a Website recommending famous restaurants and dishes, has recently become popular. You can easily find the most famous dishes of a restaurant on that Website.

找不着北 (zhǎo bù zháo běi)
lose one's bearings

It is a colloquial expression commonly used to refer

to someone being baffled by a confusing situation or snapped by overwhelming rivals.

蛰居族 (zhé jū zú)
secluded clan

Compared with the group of NEET — Not in Employment, Education or Training — these people go further. The secluded clan refers to some young people who do not work, live off their parents and stay at home all the time to avoid any social life or contact with other people.

真人秀 (zhēn rén xiù)
reality show

It refers to TV programs which feature common people caught in real life situations instead of acting as the producer directs.

枕边风 (zhěn biān fēng)
pillow talk

This term refers specifically to the private conversions between a husband and wife in China. The "pillowside breeze," as the Chinese term translates literally, usually describes a situation where a wife tries to influence her husband's decisions through gentle whispers in the bed.

震撼 (zhèn hàn)
shocked, dumbfounded

As a general tendency, Netizens love to use powerful or exaggerated words and phrases to express their feelings. So, they usually employ this Chinese phrase meaning literally "shocking" or "shocked" to say that they are surprised.

正太控 (zhèng tài kòng)
shota complex

The word "shota," derived from Japanese cartoons, refers to those thin and weak Asian boys aged between 3 to 13 years old usually in shorts. Some people, mostly females, take a fancy to comics and stories featuring such characters and pay extra attention to them. They are known to have a shota complex.

职客 (zhí kè)
job-hunting agent

A term used to refer to those who help others find a job and then charge a certain amount as a fee. This kind of self-employed agent sees a job-wanted post on the Internet and helps find one as specified by using their connections as well as job market information.

直升机父母(zhí shēng jī fù mǔ)
helicopter parents

The term refers to parents who are always obsessively worried about their children's future and safety and prefer to do everything for them. They are hovering over their children like helicopters, watchful and noisy.

植物人 (zhí wù rén)
plant lover

It is used these days in reference to eco-conscious people who like to grow plants near their homes. The Chinese term literally means a person in a comatose state.

职业舞伴 (zhí yè wǔ bàn)
taxi dancer

Paramount, one of the oldest entertainment venues in Shanghai, began recruiting professional "taxi dancers" recently, to dance with guests and guide them.

纸黄金 (zhǐ huáng jīn)
paper gold

A general term to describe gold contrasts, which do not necessarily involve the delivery of physical gold. The International Monetary Fund invented "paper gold" in 1971. The Bank of China Shanghai branch now sells paper gold 24 hours a day.

纸枷锁 (zhǐ jiā suǒ)
paper yoke

n ancient China, some offenders were shackled with a pillory and made to hold a bowl of water with their enclosed hands. If they spilled the water they would be clubbed to death. Now people use paper pillory to refer to subtle oppression one may face in life.

纸片人 (zhǐ piàn rén)
paper man

Many girls dream to have a super slim body, just as thin as a piece of paper. So, this term is often used to describe anyone who is sadly underweight. It may also mean someone who is sensitive and fragile.

纸馅包子 (zhǐ xiàn bāo zi)
cardboard bun

It refers to steamed buns stuffed with a mixture of minced pork and cardboard pulp. Beijing TV Station has been widely criticized for fabricating a "news" story about a Beijing vendor selling steamed buns with cardboard stuffing.

致命垃圾 (zhì mìng lā jī)
killer litter

See "高楼掷物" (gāo lóu zhì wù) on page 104.

钟摆族 (zhōng bǎi zú)
pendulum clan

This term refers to those young white-collar workers who travel a long distance between their offices and homes in the Yangtze River Delta area. It usually takes at least two hours to go from one place to another by train, bus or car.

钟点房 (zhōng diǎn fáng)
hour-rate room, love hotel

More and more "love hotels" have mushroomed around universities in the city. These hotel rooms are usually priced by the hour. Such hotels are often patronized by students. There's also another kind of hour-rate hotel rooms in airports, which are designed for passengers who have to wait several hours between two flights.

中国宇航员 (zhōng guó yǔ háng yuán)
taikonaut

This is a hybrid word formed from the Chinese *taikong*, "space," and Greek *nautes*, "sailor." It distinguishes Chinese spacemen from the astronauts of the United States, cosmonauts of Russia and spationauts from French-speaking countires.

中美国 (zhōng měi guó)
Chimerica

According to chaos theory, a single butterfly flapping its wings in the Amazonian jungle may cause a hurricane in Manhattan. In the global economy, this symptom is called "Chimerica," a new portmanteau word that combines "China" and "America," indicating that the two countries share a dependence on one economy, with each side interactive and complementary.

种源农业 (zhǒng yuán nóng yè)
seed variety cultivation

Plant varieties and seed cultivation are an important part of the so-called modern metropolitan agriculture that has been listed as a major goal of the city in developing its rural areas in the following five years.

众包 (zhòng bāo)
crowdsourcing

This Chinese term is actually a translation of the new English word "crowdsourcing," which means obtaining labor, products, or content from people outside a company, particularly from a large group of customers or amateurs who work for little or no pay.

种草莓 (zhòng cǎo méi)
give a hickey

The term, meaning literally "planting strawberry" in Chinese, refers to the behavior of giving the skin a reddish mark through amorous kissing.

中招 (zhòng zhāo)
rise to the bait, hit by virus

The Chinese term usually refers to someone who is caught in a trap set up for him. Now, it is often used to mean that a computer is hit by virus and becomes dysfunctional.

诛三 (zhū sān)
banish the mistress

This term refers to some wives' efforts to force mistresses to leave their husbands. The term comes from *zhuxian*, meaning "killing fairies," which became popular after a fiction based on this topic became a bestseller. The word *zhu* means "kill" in Chinese, and the word *san* (three or third) implies mistress, since the "other woman" is often deemed as "the third party" in Chinese.

主旋律 (zhǔ xuán lǜ)
mainstream ideology or trend

The Chinese term borrows from musicology, which literally means the "key melody." It is now often used to stand for the mainstream (or government-backed) ideology or trend.

主张厌食者 (zhǔ zhāng yàn shí zhě)
pro-ana

This Chinese term derives from the English word pro-ana, a conjunction of the prefix "pro" (in favor of) and "ana" (short for anorexia). It refers to people who support anorexia as a kind of lifestyle.

住车族 (zhù chē zú)
car living people

It refers to some people in California who live in their cars as they have lost jobs and cannot afford rent for housing.

住家男人 (zhù jiā nán rén)
house-husband

A small proportion of married men in large cities quit their job to stay home doing all the chores and taking care of the child, as their wives usually have high-paying jobs.

注水剧 (zhù shuǐ jù)
soaked soap

These days many soap opera producers are accused of dragging out a plot into an unreasonable length in order to sell the series for a higher price to TV stations.

抓辫子 (zhuā biàn zi)
catch someone's mistake

The Chinese term translates literally "pigtail gripping." It used to be a crucial tactic in winning the upper hand in a bare-hand fight during the Qing dynasty, when every man had to keep a pigtail on the back of his head. Nowadays, however, the term is often used to mean picking out and catching someone's mistakes, particularly in political campaigns.

抓狂 (zhuā kuáng)
going crazy

Young people these days often use this term to describe a person who is behaving insanely because he is so mad at something or he has lost control of a grim situation.

拽 (zhuǎi)
arrogant

The word originates from a northern dialect but has come into use in daily talk these days to mean those who pride themselves on skills, fame, or income over their rivals or peers.

装嫩族 (zhuāng nèn zú)
grups

Grups refers to people who are in their 30s or 40s but act like they're in their 20s. They have been credited with killing off the generation gap as they redefine age. This word originated from a New York magazine that described a "Star Trek" episode featuring a planet run by wild children trapped in perpetual youth. The children call "Captain Kirk" and his crew grups, short for grown-ups.

装修房 (zhuāng xiū fáng)
finished apartment

The city plans to promote marketing of more finished apartments, complete with flooring, bathroom and kitchen units and painted walls and windows, in an attempt to cut down noise pollution and prevent destruction of residential buildings resulting from individuals' random plans of installing equipment in and decorating their new homes.

撞色 (zhuàng sè)
color clash

Some fashion fans are promoting the intentional match of clothing and accessories in colors that are normally considered to be a poor match because of too-drastic differences or too-similar bright or dark tones.

撞衫 (zhuàng shān)
clothing clashing

This Chinese term means two or more people appear in a gathering or a public place accidentally wearing identical clothing. So, all fashion-minded ladies would try their very best to avoid *zhuangshan* or "clothing clashing." For them, clothing clashing is a disaster or an embarrassment, to say the least.

追星族 (zhuī xīng zú)
star chaser, groupie

The recent suicide of the father of a young woman who is an admirer of Hong Kong pop star Andy Lau points to the concern of the psychological health of some fans of big stars.

子弹头列车 (zǐ dàn tóu liè chē)
bullet train

Bullet trains are trains with bullet-shaped locomotives, which are designed according to aerodynamics, allowing the train to run at a high speed. A bullet train arrived in Shanghai on January 15, which will travel between 200 and 250 kilometers an hour.

紫领 (zǐ lǐng)
purple-collar

The people in this group have the brains of the white-collar and the skills of the blue-collar. They are practical, progressive and have unrivaled personal presence that earns them far more income than white-collars and golden-collars combined.

自闭症儿童 (zì bì zhèng ér tóng)
autistic child

There are reportedly more than 10,000 children suffering from autism in Shanghai and there is no known cure. Japan recently donated US$80,000 to a Shanghai kindergarten to improve the treatment for such children.

自来熟 (zì lái shú)
naturally chummy, gregarious

It refers to people who tend to willingly and instantly befriend strangers or newcomers. Some people like this kind of "instant befriending" attitude, but others loathe it.

自然醒 (zì rán xǐng)
wake-up naturally

How urban employees wish to wake up with their bio-clock, not the alarm clock! But under the pressure of fast-paced city life, having a sound sleep and waking up naturally has become a luxury for many urban workers.

自由行 (zì yóu xíng)
self-guided tour

This has become an increasingly popular form of travel with urban residents in China, especially among the young people. Having hotel and transport arranged by travel agencies and the itinerary totally controlled in their own hands, the travelers can enjoy the convenience of a package tour and the freedom of backpacking travel.

自助自行车 (zì zhù zì xíng chē)
self-service bicycle rental

The self-service bicycle rental service has been introduced into a few cities around the country to ease road congestion and cut emissions.

走光 (zǒu guāng)
wardrobe malfunction

This is a euphemism to describe an accidental exposure of some intimate parts of human body. For instance, Janet Jackson blamed her scandalous breakaway dress in her Super Bowl performance in 2004 on a "wardrobe malfunction."

走鬼 (zǒu guǐ)
illegal booth owner

This term is mostly used in Guangdong, which means people who run illegal stalls along the streets and play hide-and-seek with police officers. The owners have to push their booths and escape as fast as possible to avoid being caught by police. The Chinese term literally means "walking ghost."

走过场 (zǒu guò chǎng)
go through the motions

This Chinese term, literally "Walk through," means doing things perfunctorily, or merely pretending to do it. Many people say that some public hearings concerning their direct interests organized by local governments are just being held for the sake of holding it.

走婚族 (zǒu hūn zú)
weekend spouses

Some young couples in large Chinese cities live with their respective parents during the working week and live together in their own home only at weekends. The expression comes from a tradition in some matriarchal areas of Yunnan Province where a grown-up woman can invite men to live with her and dismisses them after a child is born.

走穴 (zǒu xuè)
moonlighting

This term refers specially to actors, actresses or singers and doctors, lecturers or engineers who use their own time to work in something that is not arranged by their employers or take a second or third job for additional income.

租奴 (zū nú)
house–rent slave

Some people in big cities like Beijing and Shanghai, especially those young workers from other provinces, have to take out a big part of their salary to pay their rent.

足球寡妇 (zú qiú guǎ fù)
football widow

Not everyone is thrilled about the World Cup, especially the wives of feverish football fans. With shopping discounts and traveling specials offered by sharp-sighted business people, these women will manage through this difficult month.

组合拳 (zǔ hé quán)
policy package, joint action

It refers to the practice of resorting to a package of policies or tactics or a multi-prong approach to tackle a specific issue. The term derives from the sport expression of combination blow in kung fu and boxing.

钻石王老五 (zuàn shí wáng lǎo wǔ)
diamond bachelor

The Chinese term translates directly as "an old Joe with diamonds." A diamond bachelor has usually passed the optimum marriage years, but is much valued because he is successful in his career and has status in society. Many women desire such bachelors.

作女 (zuō nǚ)
high-maintenance woman

Such women need a lot of care and attention from a partner. Men usually have to spend a lot of money to maintain their relationship because these women tend to have an endless stream of demands.

作弊克 (zuò bì kè)
anti-cheat sensor

China's education authorities have installed such electronic devices in many schools to prevent examinees cheating via wireless radio signal receivers. The sensor is able to pinpoint dishonest examinees who use an earphone or any other receiver to obtain answers to the exam.

坐家 (zuò jiā)
sedentary worker

This Chinese term, implying a "chair-bound professional," refers to sedentary workers, such as typists, computer operators and paper pushers.

做派 (zuò pài)
acting, way of behavior

This term originally means the acting or gestures and movements on stage. Now, it is also used to depict a person's way of behavior or manner in doing things or dealing with various situations and people.

做秀 (zuò xiù)
publicity stunt

The term means some exaggerated or unusual behaviors people do to draw public attention to promote themselves, products or anything else. East China Normal University reportedly questioned a housekeeping service company's recent attempt to hire students as temporary *ayi* was a publicity stunt.
